THE HOLY SPIRIT

GIVER of LIFE
GIVER of POWER
GIVER of GIFTS

Dr. Clark Peddicord

A HANDBOOK FOR PERSONAL
AND COMMUNITY GROWTH

PHILOSOPHIA
INTERNATIONAL

THE HOLY SPIRIT: GIVER of LIFE, GIVER of POWER, GIVER of GIFTS

First Edition May 2021
(Pentecost Week)

© 2021 Clark Herbert Peddicord

Cover created by Roy DeYoung

Library of Congress Control Number (LCCN): 2021933119

Paperback ISBN: 978-1-7333495-2-9

Published by Philosophia International Inc.
Boise, ID U.S.A.

For Samuel, Aviyah and...

TABLE OF CONTENTS

Introduction:
User's Guide

INTRODUCTION
User's Guide

Why a "handbook" about the Holy Spirit?

In God's history with his people the renewal of spiritual life is closely associated with listening to Scripture: the ancient faith-documents of Israel and the message of the Church of Jesus Christ as found in the Bible. This will always be true for the family of God.

Careful and comprehensive Bible study can help us to better grasp the significance of the Holy Spirit for human and salvation history. We can come to a deeper understanding of the Holy Spirit and his work among us as we develop a living relationship with him through the Word of God.

Every Sunday, Christians solemnly confess their faith as they speak the Apostle's Creed: "I believe in the Holy Spirit..." But many, though they take their faith seriously, do not have a clear comprehension of this Holy Spirit. They are much like the followers of John the Baptist in the ancient city of Ephesus. "Did you receive the Holy Spirit when you believed?" the Apostle Paul asked. Their answer was one many might give today: "They spoke to him: No, we have not even heard that there is a Holy Spirit!" (Acts 19)

This study is intended to help clarify central issues concerning the Holy Spirit and to enable a deeper understanding of who he is and why he has come. It is a study guide and handbook for personal and community spiritual growth.

What does this handbook offer?

The Holy Spirit: Giver of Life, Giver of Power, Giver of Gifts is written to help believers become more familiar with the Scriptural foundation of our faith regarding the Holy Spirit and experience the reality of the Spirit in our lives.

It can also be used as a leader's guide for a small group Bible study or discussion group in churches and spiritual communities.

It is a guidebook that can provide help those who want to develop a more solid foundation regarding their faith and understanding of their life with God.

About Bible Translations

There are several distinct approaches to modern Bible translation. Briefly, these are: *formally equivalent translations* (these aim at the closest possible grammatical agreement between the original and its translation in the "target" language); *dynamic equivalent translations* (these are committed to "agreement in meaning" rather than strict grammatical equivalence); and *conceptually equivalent translations* (these aim at having an impact in the target culture like the original did in its culture and time). Each approach embodies a different working strategy or goal that in turn arises from a specific philosophy of translation. (It is worth mentioning in passing that each type of translation also carries with it typical problems. But that discussion would lead us far beyond the framework of this guidebook.)

Formally equivalent translations are useful for serious Bible study because they allow an English-speaking reader to approach as closely as possible the structure and arrangement of the original Greek or Hebrew text and catch many of the similarities and relationships between words and phrases that are at home in the original. Because of this, we've chosen to use the English Standard Version (ESV), a formally equivalent translation.

One more detail that weighed in for our choice of the ESV translation is that the actual Greek and Hebrew text that the translators used is the best that modern textual research can provide. It is probably worth buying a personal copy of the ESV to use alongside this guidebook.

How is this handbook put together?

There are ten chapters, each of which is made up of 5 parts. Each part is indicated by a specific symbol.

Orientation
Opens up the topic and leads us into the biblical text.

Connection
Gives background information and links the topic of the study with a broader biblical and historical framework.

Exploration
Here we gain insights from the Scriptures of the Hebrew Bible and the New Testament. This is the heart of each study unit. Specific questions are designed to help lead to a deeper personal investigation of the Bible.

Growth
Here the insights we gain are connected to the questions, needs and problems of our daily life. We consider and meditate on how the truth we have discovered connects to our personal world.

Wisdom
We listen and reflect on how our fathers and mothers in the Faith understood the Scriptures and try to learn from these teachers and sages how to better understand and accurately interpret the Bible.

The Gender of the Spirit

The Holy Spirit does not fit easily into most of our familiar categories for God and things eternal. In the Hebrew Bible, the Spirit chooses to use people that most pious folk would find extremely "sketchy". Take Samson, for example. One of the great judges of Israel, he was a bawdy, brawling street fighter whose eye roved far from the chaste daughters of Israel. He ended up falling victim to his enemies, but God's Spirit did not completely abandon him and he ended his life eliminating hundreds of his torturers and destroying their temple. A strange choice for God's Spirit to make.

Then there is the issue of the Spirit's "gender". The exact nature of God's Spirit was always a bit ambiguous for Israel. Was the Spirit, in fact, the Eternal himself, or a sort of manifestation of God – like an "aura" that glowed when God was near? And, as time went on, Israel associated the Spirit more and more directly with Wisdom, cooperating with God in making the earth, laughing with delight and dancing before him. (Book of Proverbs, chapter 8.) As time passed, Israel associated Wisdom more and more directly with the female element of life. So, quite naturally, the Spirit also began to be more gender-ambiguous. This tendency only increased in the centuries just before Christ, when Israel learned to speak Greek and call Wisdom "*Sophia*" – a word in the "feminine" gender in Greek.

With this observation we are deep in the thicket of the modern arguments. This short study guide is not going to cut the knot and solve all the conflicts and discussion. That is not its purpose. But since we've opened Pandora's box, we should take just a moment to at least hint at how one could approach these questions.

Very simply put, from ancient times Israel recognized that there were certain categories of worship and ways of talking about God that were "off limits". There was plenty of gender variety in the pantheons of the nations around Israel and sexual activity was an active part of "worship" in many pagan rites. But Israelite religion built a wall against this. The prophets and teachers of the nation (when they weren't themselves compromised) consistently made clear: This is not a legitimate way to worship and honor the Eternal!

Simply stated, Israel was authorized to speak of God and imagine him only in the masculine gender. Of course, this fit in with a highly patriarchal structure of society. But there was also the underlying issue: Israel had seen how "crazy" and evil things got when sex and gender ambiguity was mixed with religion.

And yet, as the centuries rolled on toward the time when Jesus was born, there was always the provocative, enigmatic figure of Wisdom in the background – hinting that while there are boundaries about how we should worship God, "He" does not fit entirely within our simple and elemental categories. The Spirit represents the "unpredictable" in the Eternal, the uncontrollable reality of God. The Spirit reminds us that we do not have God captured in our categories or boxed in by our doctrines. Doctrines and Creeds are important and have their place. They are like the guard-rails on a mountain road. But the Spirit is the Life-Giver, the generator of "randomness".

So, while this study will quite often use the traditional pronoun of "He" for the Spirit, we should keep in mind that God will never fit entirely into our framework and metaphors and if we focus closely on the story of creation, we can catch a glimpse of a powerful figure wrapped in light, laughing and dancing with delight before God at the world they'd made, "rejoicing in his inhabited world and delighting in the children of man." (Proverbs 8)

רוּחַ־אֵל עָשָׂתְנִי
וְנִשְׁמַת שַׁדַּי תְּחַיֵּנִי

סִפְרֵי אִיּוֹב

"The Spirit of God has made me, and the breath of the Almighty gives me life."

Job 33:4

GIVER OF LIFE

The Holy Spirit in
Creation and History

Chapter 1
The Creator Spirit:
Lord and Life-Giver

Orientation

Wind can be an incredibly powerful force. Anyone who has experienced a tornado or hurricane will confirm this! The people of the Bible were even more vulnerable to the power of the wind than we are today. In the desert, the wind would suddenly appear as if out of nowhere, almost like a living being with its own will. A cool wind was refreshing for field laborers working under the blistering heat of the sun; a sudden storm could blow down a tent or level a house constructed of mud and clay. In light of this, it is not surprising that Israel began to associate the wind with the power of God very early in its history. Much later, Jesus made use of the image of the wind in a conversation with a leading Rabbi:

> "The wind blows where it wishes, and you hear its sound, but you do not know where it comes from or where it goes. So it is with everyone who is born of the Spirit."
>
> Gospel of John 3:8

The early Christians' understanding of God's Spirit and his work in creation and history was deeply rooted in the Hebrew Bible. In the first two chapters of this study we will explore Israel's understanding of the Spirit of God in order to establish a foundation for understanding the teachings of Jesus and the Church.

Connection

Israel was completely convinced that God is the actual source of all life and power in the entire universe. Due to the fact that in Hebrew (the language of Israel and the Hebrew Bible) the same word is used for wind as for spirit, it is no surprise that the two became associated with one another.

1. What is the relationship between God's "breath" and human life according to Genesis 2:7?

2. How did God use the wind as his instrument in order:
   • to renew the earth after the flood (Genesis 8:1)?

   • to save the people of Israel when they were escaping from Egypt (Exodus 14:21–22)?

3. What is the connection that Israel made between God's "breath" or the "wind" of God and his work in creating life (Psalm 33:6, 9; Psalm 104:30)?

4. According to the book of Job what would have been the consequences if God's Spirit were no longer working in the world (Job 34:12–15)?

Exploration

The Spirit of God and the Power of God

In the Hebrew Bible, God's Spirit is often seen in connection with the *power* of God.

> 5. According to Isaiah 63:11–14 how did God's Spirit help the people of God during their exodus from Egypt?

> 6. What image is used in connection with God's Spirit in v. 12 of Isaiah 63? Why is this a particularly appropriate picture of God's power?

The Hebrew language makes use of many metaphors (verbal pictures). Phrases such as "the hand (or arm) of God" refer to his power. The book of the prophet Ezekiel uses other striking metaphors in association with the Spirit of God (Ezekiel 3:14; 8:1–3; 37:1).

Israel also saw a sign of the work of God's Spirit in the extraordinary power of its heroes and deliverers ("judges").

> 7. How did God's Spirit work in the lives of the "judges" of Israel? (See the Book of Judges in the Hebrew Bible.)

- Othniel (Judges 3:9–11)?

- Gideon (Judges 6:34)?

- Samson (Judges 14:5–6, 19; 15:14–15)?

The Hebrew language, with its vivid imagery, illustrates quite graphically the absolute power and authority of the Spirit. In some translations of these passages one finds the expression: "The Spirit of the Lord filled (him)." Martin Buber, the Jewish philosopher, attempts to capture the meaning of this phrase with the following translation: "The Spirit of God clothed himself with… (the person)." God's Holy Spirit isn't at our beck and call. The Spirit doesn't simply come at our call in a "healing service" or anywhere else. The Spirit is the divinely sovereign LORD of creation and acts when and where he wills.

The Spirit and Wisdom

Israel also associated God's Spirit with wisdom long before the time of Jesus and the Apostles. This connection emphasizes the personal dimension of the Spirit (cf. Proverbs 8:22–31). Israel believed that God's "breath" or Spirit reveals the purpose of God in history. His Spirit guides and moves history in such a way that God's objectives are reached. Even individuals outside the covenant of Israel are employed in order to accomplish the will of God.

The nations in the Bible – both Israel and the Gentiles (*goyim*) – recognized that some people have an exceptional portion of wisdom and insight. Such men and women were considered to be special friends and instruments of God (or, if they were in a gentile culture: of the *gods*). In the narratives of Israel's patriarchs in Genesis we read of Joseph, the Hebrew slave who saved the Egyptian empire from catastrophe.

8. What was the source of Joseph's wisdom according to the Egyptian Pharaoh (Genesis 41:37–38)?

9. According to Pharaoh, what role does God play in the deliverance from the predicted famine (Genesis 41:39)?

Numbers 22–24 describe how Balaam, a Gentile magician, is commissioned by an enemy of Israel to put a curse on the people of God. Instead, God's Spirit overcomes Balaam and compels him to bless Israel.

> 10. How does Numbers 24:1–4 describe Balaam's encounter with the Spirit of God (esp. vv. 3–4)?

Growth

The people of Israel recognized in God's Creator-Spirit, his *ruach* ("breath"), the power of life in nature (Ps 33:6, 9; Ps 104:24–30). They looked forward to the time when this same Spirit would work in an exceptional way in the life of the *Messiah* ("Anointed One"), a promised deliverer whose coming was foretold by the prophets. As we'll see later, Jesus unambiguously declared that these prophecies were fulfilled in his life and work. He claimed a special connection to the Spirit of God.

> 11. Knowing that the Spirit that was in Jesus created the life, beauty and order we see in the universe, how should a follower of Jesus relate to the world of nature and the environment around us?

The Spirit of God, who created order out of original chaos, wants to bring about beauty and harmony in the life of every person.

> 12. Are there areas of your life in which you desire a portion of this creative/artistic/healing power of the Spirit of God?

Wisdom

From the beginning of Israel's history with God, the people of God have attempted to summarize their faith in "confessions" – short texts consisting of a few precise, powerful statements. The best known of Israel's faith statements, the *Shema*, illustrates this: "Hear (*shema*), O Israel: The Lord our God, the Lord is one." (Deuteronomy 6:4)

In keeping with this tradition, Christians also agreed throughout the history of the church to a number of key faith statements or "confessions". These have, in the meantime, become the central *creeds* of the church. For example, the so-called *Nicene Creed* is considered more or less authoritative by and for all Christians. (It was formulated in the town of Nicea by a council of bishops – an assembly of the leading teachers and thinkers of all Christendom – three hundred years after the time of Jesus.)

In the *Nicene Creed* it says: "We believe in the Holy Spirit, the Lord who gives life …". In the original Greek text (and in newer translations) it says: "the Holy Spirit (is) *Lord and Life-giver*". This is a good summary of what we have seen in this chapter. It also fulfills the task of a creed: to briefly assert the essentials about how the people of God understand Holy Scripture on a specific topic. The creeds of the faith do not replace the Bible, but rather offer the people of God a guideline for the correct understanding of the Bible: "This is how our fathers and mothers in the faith understood the Holy Scripture!"

Chapter 2
The God who Speaks

 *Orientation*

Israel was convinced that God had entered into a covenant – a binding contract – with her in order to accomplish his objectives in history. He called Abraham away from house and home and invited him into a personal covenant relationship with himself, the living God. He liberated Israel from Egyptian bondage and, on Mt. Sinai, made a covenant with the nation and gave them his instructions and commission (*Torah*).

In Chapter 1 we saw how God directly intervened on behalf of his people and warded off their enemies by supernaturally empowering certain heroic individuals ("Judges") with his Spirit in specific places and at specific times for specific tasks. But rather than simply playing the role of a kind of hero-warrior, these men and women also usually gave their people guidance and leadership through wise counsel and concrete actions.

In this chapter we will explore how Israel's understanding of God and his ways grew over time. We will focus our attention particularly on the question: How did God lead his people as well as communicate his goals and purposes to them?

Connection

Although Israel believed that God's Spirit was generally active in the world in various ways, she was deeply convinced that he revealed his will most clearly in, to and through *his chosen people, Israel*. The book of Nehemiah was written after the experience of Israel in Babylonian exile. In chapter 9 the author reflects back on this history.

1. According to Nehemiah 9:20 why did God give Israel his Spirit during their exodus from Egypt and during their 40 years of wandering in the wilderness?

2. In Numbers 11:16–17 an event that occurred during the wilderness experience is described. Why did God give the large group of tribal leaders his Spirit?

3. According to Numbers 11:25–30 what was Moses' wish for the entire nation of Israel?

4. Through whom did God repeatedly make his will for Israel known according to Nehemiah 9:30?

The Book of 2 Samuel describes the influence of God's Spirit upon David, Israel's great military leader, king and songwriter.

5. What was the connection between God's Spirit and the words and actions of David (2 Samuel 23:1–4)?

Exploration

The Coming Deliverer: the Person of the Spirit

Several centuries of God's history with Israel had already passed by the time the prophet Isaiah spoke for the first time of a promised deliverer who would liberate the nation from bondage. Isaiah's reference to the coming *Messiah* ("Anointed One") came right as Israel was being attacked by Assyria, at that time the most powerful military force in the world. According to the prophecy of Isaiah, the promised deliverer would be uniquely filled and led by the Spirit of God.

6. How was the presence of God's Spirit going to express itself in the life of the promised deliverer according to Isaiah 11:1–3?

With the passing of time it became clear to Israel through her prophets that the Spirit-filled Anointed One (the *Messiah*) would accomplish an outstanding, mighty work and would deliver a unique message.

7. What would be the message of the Promised One according to Isaiah 61:1–2?

CHAPTER 2: THE GOD WHO SPEAKS

The Spirit of God, the Creator Spirit, who gives and sustains life, was active in a unique way in the life and ministry of Jesus. The same Spirit, who made order out of chaos, who created everything from nothing (Genesis 1:2), worked in and through Jesus in order to bring suffering and oppressed individuals healing and new life.

Soon after he began his public ministry, Jesus was invited to do the traditional Scripture reading (*haftarah*) during a synagogue worship service. He read the passage from the book of Isaiah just mentioned. When he finished, though, he said (Luke 4:21): "Today this scripture has been fulfilled in your hearing." In doing so, Jesus was claiming to be the promised Deliverer of Israel, empowered and fully authorized by the Spirit of God.

The Absence of the Spirit – the Promise of the Spirit

The Spirit of God led his people through prophets inspired by him. This fact is foundational for Israel's faith and for that of the Church of Jesus Christ. But Israel sensed that subsequent to the prophets Haggai, Zechariah, and Malachi, to a certain extent God withdrew his Spirit. In the historical records of the books of *1 and 2 Maccabees* (the story of Jewish freedom fighters who fought against the Greco-Syrian regime a century and a half before Jesus) one reads that "the Jewish nation and its priests agreed that Simon would always be their ruler and high priest as long as and until God would raise up a true prophet amongst them" (1 Maccabees 14:41). In the short book entitled the *Apocalypse of Baruch* the author complains: "The righteous have gone to their fathers and the prophets have fallen asleep." But Israel never lost the hope of a direct and personal encounter with God in the life of every individual.

> 8. How had the Prophet Jeremiah described this hope (Jeremiah 31:31–33)?

In Chapter 36 of the book of the Prophet Ezekiel we find an important parallel to the assertion in Jeremiah.

9. How does the Prophet say that the Spirit of God will work in the hearts of the people (Ezekiel 36:26–27)?

10. The prophet Joel speaks to the same issue. How will God act in the lives of his people according to Joel 2:28–32?

Growth

Israel had long hoped for a new and deeper intervention of God's Spirit. But the years passed and the promise went unfulfilled. The clear proclamation of the prophets disappeared from Israel. The Psalmist laments: "No prophets are left, and there is not one among us who knows anything." (Psalm 74:9).

11. According to the prophet Zechariah, what was the central problem (Zechariah 7:9–12)?

12. Do you see a parallel to the present-day situation in the church or in your own life? If so, in what way?

Wisdom

In this chapter we have seen that the Spirit of God's role in the work of salvation is to give us insight about God, the world and the condition of humankind.

In the first chapter we reflected on the significance of faith creeds. These summaries assist us in coming to a deeper and more adequate, appropriate understanding of Holy Scripture. They have the potential to draw our attention to new, perhaps previously overlooked details and perspectives.

The Spirit of God connects the work of creation and the work of salvation. God's action in *creation* consists of his work through which he created the universe from nothing by his word, and he sustains it by his will and power. His action of *salvation* is his work that he does to forgive sin and bring individuals into a personal relationship with himself.

The *Nicene Creed* connects this saving work of God to the Holy Spirit with the assertion that the Holy Spirit is not only the "Life-giver", but he also "has spoken through the prophets." This reflects the New Testament perspective: "For no prophecy was ever produced by the will of man, but men spoke from God as they were carried along by the Holy Spirit." (2 Peter 1:21)

"Λήμψεσθε δύναμιν ἐπελθόντος τοῦ ἁγίου πνεύματος ἐφ᾽ ὑμᾶς καὶ ἔσεσθέ μου μάρτυρες ἔν τε Ἰερουσαλὴμ καὶ [ἐν] πάσῃ τῇ Ἰουδαίᾳ καὶ Σαμαρείᾳ καὶ ἕως ἐσχάτου τῆς γῆς."

"You will receive power when the Holy Spirit has come upon you, and you will be my witnesses... to the end of the earth."

Jesus – Acts 1:8

GIVER OF POWER

The Holy Spirit
and the Believer

Chapter 3
Jesus and the
Spirit of God

Orientation

The stories about Jesus in the Bible all emphasize his unique authority. All Jesus taught and did was characterized by an extraordinary sense of confidence and certainty.

The prophets of Israel proclaimed that the authority of God's Word would never fade away. Nature in its entirety and all human life will pass away, but "the word of our God will stand forever." (Isaiah 40:8) Jesus made the astonishing parallel claim, "heaven and earth will pass away, but *my* words will not pass away." (Mark 13:31)

It was customary in the time of Jesus for the rabbis (teachers of Scripture) to introduce and support their interpretations with the words, "Thus says the Lord…". They did this in order to emphasize the authority of their instruction. With this statement they aligned themselves with the prophets of old, whom God had sent to his people. Jesus, on the other hand, claimed a much greater and more direct authority for himself. He said: "Truly, *I* say unto you…". He would place his own statements in contrast to the interpretation of others with the words: "You have heard, that it has been said… but *I* say unto you…".

Jesus was very certain about what he thought and taught. He made the extraordinary claim that his own words are the actual foundation for all life and the standard by which people will be judged on the last day (Mark 8:38). In the Gospels we read of the response of his hearers to his instruction. They "were astonished at his teaching, for he taught them as one who had authority, and not as the scribes." (Mark 1:22)

Connection

What was the origin of Jesus' remarkable confidence and authority? Clearly, at the core of his self-identity was the assurance that he was the Son of God. He was deeply convinced that his relationship to God was special and, indeed, unique. Matthew 11:27 is a clear expression of Jesus' self-understanding: "All things have been handed over to me by my Father, and no one knows the Son except the Father, and no one knows the Father except the Son and anyone to whom the Son chooses to reveal him." However, there is also one other feature incorporated in Jesus self-understanding. He liberated individuals from their bondage stemming from and caused by the "powers of darkness". In the Synoptic Gospels (Matthew, Mark, and Luke) we read that this healing ministry triggered accusations and was met by the vehement criticism of his opponents. On at least one occasion they accused him of having received his ability to cast out demons from the "prince of demons" himself.

1. What does Jesus' response imply is the true source of his power (Mark 3:28–30)?

Jesus was convinced that his exorcisms (the casting out of demons) were an overwhelming confirmation of the presence of the Spirit of God in his life and work. The long "drought" characterized by the absence of the Spirit in Israel was coming to an end. The Spirit of God was once again active among his people.

2. Compare Luke 11:20 with Matthew 12:28. How does the text in Matthew shed light on the true source of power behind Jesus' ministry and mission?

3. According to these words, what was being announced in and through Jesus' exorcisms?

Exploration

The Authority and Power of Jesus

Jesus taught that in and through him something entirely new, definitive and final was happening. He was conscious of the fact that God's Spirit was compellingly and powerfully present in his life and in his actions. God's Spirit was active once again in Israel, and that was a sign of the coming kingdom of God.

The "kingdom of God" is an expression Israel used to describe the promised new era, in which God's reign or leadership was going to be a visible reality for all people. In the first two chapters we saw that Israel believed God's Spirit filled and empowered (took control of) individuals ("God's Spirit clothed himself with Gideon") and enabled them to speak as prophets or as wise men or women inspired by God. A sign of this new age of the Spirit would be God's pouring out his Spirit upon *all* his people (cf. Chapter 2).

When we examine the life and ministry of Jesus, we discover that the power of God's Spirit flowed through him and became visible in his powerful actions and in his proclamation of the "Good News". This was tangible evidence of the long awaited coming of the kingdom of God for which Israel had yearned. But other aspects of this long-awaited kingdom did *not* come to pass: the old structures of power, so it seemed, remained unchanged. Israel was still not able to triumph over its enemies (= Rome!) nor did the last judgment take place.

But Jesus was so conscious and confident of the effective power of the Spirit of God in his life and ministry that he could proclaim the intervening power of the final kingdom even before the fulfillment of all these things at the end of history. For Jesus, the power of God's

Spirit was an instantly recognizable and distinctive evidence that the kingdom and rule of God was being unveiled in his life and work. Matthew 11:2–6 reports that John the Baptist sent several of his disciples to Jesus with the question: "Are you the one who was to come?" (v. 3) This question shows the confusion that Jesus caused by announcing the inauguration of the kingdom of God even though the final judgment did not take place as John had expected. Jesus answered John by saying: my ministry of deliverance and healing – the promised blessings of the last days – demonstrates that God's kingdom has indeed come. These are manifestations of salvation (Matthew 11: 4–6).

> 4. Which of Jesus' deeds, apart from *healings* and *powerful works*, did he say shows conclusively that the climax of the ages had broken through? (Matthew 11:4-5)?

Just as in the Beatitudes (Matthew 5), the blessing of salvation is demonstrated most clearly in Jesus' proclamation that the poor will participate in God's kingdom and God's offer of forgiveness and acceptance is especially extended to them.

> 5. According to Luke 4:18, what is the source of Jesus' message?

Jesus attributed his healing, liberating and preaching ministry to the poor directly to the work of God's Spirit. The Spirit of God was once again active in Israel – and this in a way like never before. The promise of the Spirit, which the Prophet Isaiah had announced, was now being fulfilled.

The Baptism of Jesus

The Gospels indicate quite clearly how important his baptism by John the Baptist in the Jordan River was to Jesus. When the religious leaders of Israel confronted Jesus regarding the origin of his authority (Mark 11:27–32), he replied to them with a counter-question:

"I will ask you one question; answer me, and I will tell you by what authority I do these things. Was the baptism of John from heaven or from man? Answer me."

Jesus was not trying to dodge their question. On the contrary, this counter-question makes it clear that for Jesus the question regarding the source or origin of his authority is integrally connected with his own baptism experience. For Jesus, his authority was formally confirmed and verified when John baptized him.

All four of the Gospels are in agreement in their account that the Spirit of God did indeed come upon Jesus at his baptism. John the Baptist was witness to this as Jesus was immersed in the Jordan along with a large group of others. What followed was a defining moment for Jesus. The Gospels report that a voice came from heaven and spoke to him. These words were clearly profoundly significant for Jesus' own self-understanding.

6. What did the voice actually say about Jesus (Mark 1:11)?

This expression comes from a passage in the book of Isaiah (Isaiah 42:1). At the time of Jesus people memorized scripture and knew extensive passages by heart. When a person quoted the beginning of a passage it was generally understood that the entire passage was being referenced.

? 7. Take a careful look at Isaiah 42:1. How does the passage continue? What vitally significant concept would Jesus have associated with this passage?

Is the Spirit a Person?

We saw in the first chapter that the Spirit of God was associated with wisdom long before the time of Jesus and to a certain extent was viewed as a personal force. This is clear in the books of the Hebrew Bible and later Jewish literature.

Throughout the centuries Israel retained a strong faith in the one invisible God, but also closely associated experiences such as the *Shekinah* (the radiant divine presence in the temple) with this One God (see Exodus 40; Ezekiel 9–11). The Shekinah-Glory was considered a manifestation of God. At the same time, it represented his actions or presence for his people. The Wisdom of God and the breath or Spirit of God are closely associated; they are God's presence and power among us and for us. The great rabbis of Israel also spoke in personal terms when referring to the Spirit. The Spirit of God taught and encouraged Israel, suffered and even conversed with God. The Spirit of God came from God and represented him in our midst, but acted in a certain sense as a separate individual, i.e., as a person, but still within the parameters set by God's own character. In the Christian New Testament, particularly in the writings of John and Paul, this tradition is further developed and clarified.

? 8. How does Jesus describe the nature of God in his conversation with the Samaritan woman in John 4:24?

When the Bible speaks about God being "Spirit", it does not mean a bodyless essence similar to the way we think of a ghost. Rather, the Bible is saying that he is the one and only living being not restricted to a single location or any one period of time. God was never *given* life – he *is* Life. As a result of such reflection, the early followers of Jesus came to the conclusion that the Spirit is a "person" (with the ability to communicate and to make decisions and to act upon them), just like the Father and the Son.

The Holy Spirit is the Spirit of Jesus

We have seen that the power of the Spirit of God, which worked in and through Jesus, was a conclusive sign – a signal of the coming of a new era in God's relationship to his people. The relationship between Jesus and the Spirit has another aspect that emerges most clearly in the Gospel of John. John recognized that the Holy Spirit of God – the "Creator Spirit" – and the Spirit of Jesus were not two independent beings or entities. They are not to be conceived of as being separate from one another. It is from this insight that the unified biblical worldview emerges, in which Jesus' messianic claims and the Jewish faith in the one God indeed belong together.

John approached the story of Jesus differently than the authors of the other three Gospels (the so-called *Synoptic* Gospels = "seeing-together"). All four have particular things they bring to the historical and theological framework of Jesus' story. But in regard to the Spirit they agree, even if they approach things from different perspectives.

> **?** 9. Which additional detail does John mention in his description of how the Holy Spirit came upon Jesus at his baptism (John 1:32)?

The author of the Gospel of John apparently wanted to emphasize the unity of the Spirit of God with Jesus during his entire earthly life and even beyond his death and resurrection for all time. (John 20:21–22)

> 10. What is promised in John 7:38–39 to those who hunger for life and come to Jesus?

The Gospel of John also intimately associates the Spirit with Jesus in the life of his followers:

> 11. How is the promise of Jesus that he will come and live in his disciples fulfilled according to John 14:15–18?

In the Gospel of John, the Holy Spirit is called the other "Helper" (or *paraclete* in the original language). This means "encourager", "advocate" or "counselor" – also in a legal sense. A *paraclete* was the spokesman for the defense in a Roman trial. With this expression, the Gospel of John emphasizes that it is not an impersonal divine power that is being referred to here, but rather a powerful personal reality:

"But the Helper, the Holy Spirit, whom the Father will send in my name, he will teach you all things and bring to your remembrance all that I have said to you." (John 14:26)

The Spirit was not only sent by the Father as the pledge of Jesus' presence; the Spirit also teaches and reminds the disciples of all that he had taught them.

> 12. What additional reason does John 16:14 mention regarding why the Holy Spirit came?

Growth

The Gospels report to us that Jesus was the Promised One who would be filled with God's Spirit. Jesus' life and work carried the unmistakable stamp of God's Spirit who worked in and through him. The Apostle John also points out that the relationship between Jesus and the Spirit was not one-way. The Spirit worked through Jesus, but Jesus promised as well that the Spirit would continue his own work and be his presence in the world. The Holy Spirit is the guarantee for the personal bond between the believer and the now ever-present Resurrected One. The Holy Spirit establishes this bond or relationship between Jesus and his followers in every new generation.

13. What would be the result of a deeper experience of the Holy Spirit in your life considering the fact that it is the task of the Holy Spirit to glorify Jesus (John 16:14)?

Wisdom

This chapter of our study touched upon several issues that raise fairly complex questions about the interpretation of Scripture. A whole series of questions connected with the relationship of the Gospels to one another is involved, particularly the relationship of the first three Gospels (Matthew, Mark and Luke) to the Gospel of John. This is not the place for an extensive discussion of these topics. But a couple of things are worth noting:

In the first half of the 20th century many theologians assumed that the intellectual setting for the Gospel of John was definitely not Jewish, but rather that it emerged from a *Greek* religious context. Concepts such as light and darkness as well as other themes seemed foreign to the form of Judaism that scholars saw in rabbinical literature. However, in the mid-twentieth century, the Dead Sea scrolls were discovered. These are the writings and biblical manuscripts collected by a Jewish religious community that lived at Qumran (on the Dead Sea near Jericho). These writings come from before the time of Jesus up until the destruction of the settlement in ca. 70 A.D. As scholars investigated these texts, it became evident that the roots of the Gospel of John reach deep into an intellectual and spiritual culture that was flourishing in the Holy Land of Jesus' day.

Until quite recently scholars have also assumed that the Gospel of John was written much later than the other gospels. This assumption is now being seriously questioned. In light of the discoveries at Qumran and other research, some biblical scholars have come to the conclusion that the Gospel of John was written quite early.

What could be the reason, then, for the very different character of the Gospel of John when contrasted with the "Synoptic" Gospels? First, it is striking that for John the ministry of Jesus in the Roman province of *Judea* is at center focus. The other gospels concentrate initially on his ministry in the more northern province of *Galilee*. Second, there is significant evidence for the existence of several *different spiritual centers for Judaism* at that time. The audience that John was addressing saw the focal point of Israel and the coming Messianic kingdom in the Jerusalem temple and its ceremonies. The focal point for the audience of the synoptic Gospels was not the Jerusalem temple, but rather the local synagogues, in which they encountered the Word of God. In light of this, it is significant that the Synoptic Gospels focused on the teachings of Jesus in the synagogue and its surroundings; John is concerned with Jesus' teaching in the context of the temple.

In addition, research on the Judaism of that time indicates that the rabbis of Israel usually reserved their *distinctive core instruction* for a small group of their closest disciples. Perhaps this was the method of instruction characteristic for the author of John and another reason for the different emphasis in the Fourth Gospel.

The issues involved are complex. These suggestions regarding possible settings for the gospels simply serve as a pointer toward some new perspectives in biblical research that are worth taking note of. We need to keep this in mind as we now launch into our study of the Holy Spirit in the four New Testament gospels.

Chapter 4
The Gift of
the Holy Spirit

Orientation

We saw before that in the history of God's dealings with Israel, the Spirit of God was not poured out on each and every believer but distinctively on people God especially elected to use: judges, prophets and a few chosen kings and others like the craftsmen and artisans who made the holy tent sanctuary ("Tabernacle") and its furniture during the Exodus from Egypt.

The great prophets of Israel, though, foretold a time when God's Spirit would work directly in and through *all* of God's covenant people. Each individual would know God directly in his or her own experience:

> "They shall all know me," promised God, "from the least of them to the greatest, declares the Lord." He would forgive the wickedness of his people and "remember their sin no more." (Jeremiah 31:34)

> God promised the Israelites languishing in exile in Babylon, "I will put my Spirit within you," (Ezekiel 36:27)

Israel never lost this hope that God's Spirit would work directly in the life of every member of the people of God. An entirely new era would some day begin, with a new relationship between God and his people, a "new covenant". Knowledge of God and his will would no longer be mediated through a few special leaders, but *all* of God's covenant community would have direct assurance that their sins are forgiven and each would know God in an immediate and personal way.

Connection

When John the Baptist appeared in Israel, his message generated great excitement. Could he be the long-awaited Promised One who would be filled with God's Spirit and usher in the new age? John denied that he was the One but indicated that he was his forerunner or herald.

Read Luke 3:16 (see also the parallel texts in the other three Gospels: Matthew 3:11, Mark 1:7–8, and John 1:33).

1. What did John the Baptist say would be the work of the One coming after him?

2. To whom was John the Baptist referring? (cf. the Gospel of John 1:33)

At the end of Luke's Gospel, there is a report of a conversation that took place between the risen Jesus and two of his disciples.

3. What did Jesus promise that he would do for his followers (Luke 24:49)?

Read the continuation of Luke's narrative in the Book of Acts 1:1–8.

4. Jesus said that his followers should wait in Jerusalem for a particular event. What was that event? (vv. 4–5)

? 5. What expressions did Jesus use to describe this coming event?

V. 4: _____ my Father promised.

V. 5: You will be _____

? 6. What did Jesus say would be the result of this taking place (v. 8)?

The age of the New Covenant predicted by the prophets was dawning – it was to be the age of the Spirit, the era when God gives his Spirit to each and every member of his people as a special gift. Luke makes clear that the Spirit did not simply inaugurate the new age and then disappear. The great silver- and goldsmiths of the past placed their unique "hallmark" on each finished piece of work. The presence of the Spirit is the *defining hallmark* of the new age. The age of the Church is the age of the Spirit.

Exploration

Pentecost

In both the Gospel of Luke and at the beginning of the book of Acts, the author carefully set the stage for understanding what was to happen on the day of Pentecost described in Acts 2: Jesus would send that which the Father promised; he would baptize his people in the Holy Spirit. Luke's presentation of the events on Pentecost fits carefully into the essential thrust of the entire book of Acts, which is clearly written as the story of the ever-expanding movement of the message of Jesus. The Gospel spread out geographically, culturally, and – above all – theologically from Jerusalem to the ends of the earth; from its cradle in Israel to the full-blown incorporation of other nationalities (the "Gentiles") into the People of God.

The command to wait for the coming of the Spirit was given to the band of disciples: they were to wait in a particular location for a particular event. (It is worth noting in passing that in the more than twenty subsequent descriptions of conversions recorded in Acts, the command to wait for the Spirit is never repeated.) And the Spirit came in power! Read the account in Acts 2:1–42.

7. What explanation did Peter give for what happened (vv. 14–18)?

8. According to vv. 32–33:
What was the role of the Father in the events at Pentecost?

The role of Jesus?

The Gift of the Spirit

9. How does Peter describe the Holy Spirit to those who responded to his preaching on Pentecost (vv. 38–39)?

The story of Peter's first preaching to Gentiles in the coastal town of Joppa is told in Acts 10–11. This presents how the message of Jesus transcended the boundaries of the Jewish culture and spread to non-Jews. Read Peter's report of the event to the Jerusalem church in Acts 11:1–18.

10. According to Peter, what happened as he had been speaking that convinced him that his Gentile hearers had true faith in Jesus (Acts 11:15; see also Acts 10:44–48)?

11. How did Peter interpret what happened? (See Acts 11:16–17; also Acts 10:45–47)?

12. According to Acts 11:18, what inner process was linked with the "baptism in the Holy Spirit"?

Growth

In the account of the conversion of three thousand on the day of Pentecost, it points out that these converts "continued in the teaching of the Apostles, in fellowship, the breaking of bread and prayer". (Acts 2:42)

Consider your life in respect to these four areas and describe briefly how you take part in the study and learning of the Scriptures (the "teaching of the Apostles"), fellowship in common worship, sharing with others, and prayer. Would you like to see change or improvement in any of these areas of your life?

Study   *Worship*

Sharing   *Prayer*

Wisdom

It is a very important principle of interpreting the Bible that one should always interpret a particular passage in light of the *context* of the book in which it stands. This provides a framework and a control for understanding the text being considered. We touched briefly in this chapter on the *purpose* of the Book of Acts – why it was composed by Luke. We saw that it is an account of the *expansion* of the Gospel, geographically, culturally, and theologically. The structure of the Book of Acts is built around this movement and that must be the framework for our understanding of any individual passages as well as the whole book.

One can often detect the purpose and framework of a book by examining its introductory section: in Acts 1, for instance, Luke places great emphasis on the words of the Risen Jesus that the witness of the disciples would extend to all the cultures and regions of the world: starting in Jerusalem, then Judea, Samaria, and to the ends of the earth (1:8). Luke follows this structure in unfolding the narrative of the rest of the book.

Another way to identify the overarching theme or themes of a book is to look for places where the writer has used other means to emphasize something.

One technique for showing emphasis is *repetition*. In Acts Chapters 1–12, Luke emphasizes the coming of the Holy Spirit by relating three times how the gift of the Spirit was given to three distinct *cultural* groups: the Jewish people (Acts 2), the Samaritans (Acts 8), and the Gentiles (Acts 10–11). He especially emphasized the coming of the Spirit on the Gentiles by first recounting the incident, then repeating all of the main points of the narrative once again in Chapter 11.

Writing material was very expensive in the first century and a narrator did not do something like this lightly. The author of Acts had to have a very particular purpose in mind. This was obviously a crucial point in the development of the theme of his book. From that point on in Acts, the emphasis on the *geographic* expansion of the Church continues outward to the nations and the major *theological* question that arose during that expansion is discussed in detail. That issue was the relationship of the Church to the law of Moses and whether Gentiles had to first become Jewish converts in order to follow Jesus (Acts 15).

Luke's focus on this *salvation-history* has important consequences for our study about the work of the Holy Spirit:

In each case where Luke mentions the initial experience of the Spirit (Acts Chapters 2, 8, 10–11, and 19), he introduces a cultural group newly touched by the expansion of the Gospel. In each of these dramatic outpourings of the Spirit, the *manifestations* of the Spirit are part of a *corporate* experience that represents a major stage in salvation-history. In none of these descriptions is the focus of attention on the experience of an *individual* convert. Thus, Luke does not present these events as a necessary model of what every *individual* believer needs to experience in receiving the Holy Spirit. That interpretation would be too individualistic and fails to take into account Luke's central focus on the progress of salvation history.

Thus, to find out what it means for *all believers* to be baptized in the Spirit or filled with the Spirit we have to turn to the places in Scripture where these topics are directly addressed. More precisely, we must look to the teaching of Jesus in the Gospels and the writings and teaching of the Apostles in the letters to the churches. The narrative sections of the Book of Acts focus on other issues. In them, Luke describes how the Gospel expanded from the Jewish culture outward to Samaria, the Gentiles, and to those who were followers of John the Baptist. His interest was in the flow of salvation-history and these narratives were *not* necessarily intended to present what is the norm for each and every believer in Jesus in all places and at all times.

Finally, in the Book of Acts, Luke also does not seem to be particularly interested in the question of where the experience of the gift of the Spirit fits in with water baptism and conversion. He does not address this issue and as a result, the question of what is the normal *sequence* of a) faith, b) water baptism and c) the gift of the Spirit cannot be answered from the Book of Acts. For an answer to that question we must turn to other places in Scripture. We investigate that in the next chapter.

CHAPTER 4: THE GIFT OF THE SPIRIT

Τῇ ἐπαύριον βλέπει
τὸν Ἰησοῦν ἐρχόμενον
πρὸς αὐτὸν καὶ λέγει...
οὗτός ἐστιν ὁ βαπτίζων
ἐν πνεύματι ἁγίῳ.

Κατα Ιωαννην 1

"The next day he saw Jesus coming toward him, and said, '…this is he who baptizes with the Holy Spirit.'"

John 1:29,33

Chapter 5
Baptism in
the Holy Spirit

Orientation

Israel anticipated that the Spirit of God would come on "all flesh" (Joel 2:28–32). This would inaugurate an entirely new age and a new relationship between God and his people. Under this "new covenant", as the prophet Jeremiah called it (Jeremiah 31:31), *all* of God's people would enjoy the gift of the "Spirit of prophecy".

This new age dawned with the events that took place on the day of Pentecost. The Apostle Peter made this clear by quoting Joel's prediction in his speech on Pentecost and then affirming "This is that which was prophesied by the prophet Joel." Moses' ancient hope was being fulfilled: "I wish that all the Lord's people were prophets and that the Lord would put his Spirit on them!" (Numbers 11:29)

It is true that Israel's special leaders such as King David or the great prophets had experienced the presence and manifestation of God's Spirit, but the day of Pentecost signaled a *new* and widely distributed experience of the Spirit. The presence of the Holy Spirit in the life of *every* believer was the decisive evidence that the age of the Messiah had begun. According to all four Gospels this was foretold by John the Baptist. He predicted that the Coming One would usher in that age by *baptizing his people in the Holy Spirit*.

Connection

Particularly in the Gospel of John, Jesus makes clear that his own departure and return to the Father is a necessary pre-condition for the coming of the Holy Spirit.

> **?** 1. According to John 16:7, why was Jesus' departure not something that his disciples should be sad about?

In the time of Jesus, the autumn festival of the *Feast of Tabernacles* (*Sukkot*) was one of the "pilgrim feasts" when believing Jews celebrated the holy days in Jerusalem. This feast commemorates the years of Israel's wandering in the desert. Shelters or "booths" made of palm branches were constructed and used for seven days. In the first century, special celebrations took place after the last day. On this "Great Day", special sacrifices were made and the booths were dismantled. The *Hallel* songs (the pilgrim Psalms 113–118) were sung repeatedly.

At daybreak on each of the holy days, water was carried in a solemn procession from the Pool of Siloam to the inner court of the temple. There it was poured out to the Lord along with the daily drink offering of wine. These water ceremonies were related in Jewish thought to the promised pouring out of God's Spirit in the last days — an anticipation of the spiritual "rains" of renewal and refreshment that would come with the age of the Messiah. According to ancient Jewish tradition (in the *gemara* to the Talmud tractate *Megilah* 31a), the Scripture reading for the "Great Day" of the feast was Deuteronomy 33, the closing section of the entire *Torah* (five books of Moses).

In that section, there is a reference to the "fountain of Jacob". The other reading of the day (the *haftarah*) was from 1 Kings 8:22: "Then Solomon stood before the altar of the Lord in the presence of all the assembly of Israel and spread out his hands toward heaven, and said…"

It was before this backdrop that Jesus made an astonishing claim:

> "On the last day of the feast, the great day, Jesus stood up and cried out, 'If anyone thirsts, let him come to me and drink. Whoever believes in me, as the Scripture has said, *Out of his heart will flow rivers of living water*.' Now this he said about the Spirit, whom those who believed in him were to receive, for as yet the Spirit had not been given, because Jesus was not yet glorified."
>
> John 7:37–39

2. According to Jesus, what is a spiritually "thirsty" person to do? (v. 37)

3. What did Jesus promise would be the result? (v. 38)

4. What was the meaning of the word-picture of "water" that Jesus used? I.e. What does water "stand for"? (v. 39)

Jesus claimed to be the *source* of the Spirit in the dawning Messianic age, the promised "Age of the Spirit".

5. According to v. 39, when would the Spirit be "given" in this way?

The Gospel of John says that the new age of the Spirit would come as a consequence of the completed work of the Son. The Gospel of John tells of a meeting between Jesus and his disciples after his death and resurrection, in which the Risen One "blew his breath" on them.

? 6. The prophets of Israel frequently did symbolic actions like this. What did Jesus' act of "breathing" on his disciples symbolize? (John 20:22)

Throughout the Gospel of John, a *preview* is often given of an event that is going to take place later. This is especially true for the statements of Jesus about his impending glorification. That is probably also the case with this episode. John's Gospel does *not* connect the fulfillment of the promises spelled out in John 14–16 with Jesus' act of breathing during this meeting with the disciples. Thus, it is likely that this was a symbolic action pointing to a fulfillment that was yet to come. There are good grounds for thinking that *Pentecost* was the reference point that John had in mind. It became a Christian feast very early and was part of the common knowledge of the early church.

Thus, Jesus' act of breathing was a kind of *acted parable* that pointed forward to the full coming of the Holy Spirit that still lay ahead for the disciples (though in the past for John's readers).

Finally, through the gift of the Spirit, the People of God would continue the ministry of Jesus, proclaiming forgiveness of sins to those who believe and judgment for those who harden their hearts (see John 20:23).

Exploration

The Gift of the Spirit = Baptism in the Spirit

Acts 10 describes the moment when God sent the gift of his Spirit for the first time upon non-Jews and incorporated them into the church. (Sometimes called the "Gentile Pentecost". We looked at this more closely in Chapter 4.) In Acts 11:15 Peter later tells the Jewish believers in Jerusalem that "the Holy Spirit fell on them (the group of Gentiles in Caesarea) as on us *at the beginning*."

For Peter, as for the other leaders of the church, the *beginning* of their real faith in Christ was linked with *their own* receiving of the

Holy Spirit, just as it was later for Cornelius the Gentile. In Acts 15 a gathering of the leaders of the church in Jerusalem is reported at which the question of the relation of Gentile believers to the Jewish ceremonial laws was discussed. After a long discussion, Peter stood to speak and referred once again to his encounter with Cornelius.

7. According to the Book of Acts, what did Cornelius and the other Gentiles with him do?

Acts 11:1 The Gentiles _____

Acts 15:7 The Gentiles _____

_____

8. What did God do to and for these Gentiles?

Acts 11:18 God has... _____

Acts 15:7–9 God chose that the Gentiles would hear the message of the Gospel...

v. 8 and "he _____ their hearts

and _____ to them by giving

them _____".

v. 9 and he "cleansed their hearts by _____".

Finally, Peter affirmed that both Jews and Gentiles "will be

saved through _____".

The New Testament uses the expression "*baptism* in the Spirit" as an equivalent to the "*gift* of the Spirit" which God had promised to give his people (Acts 11:16–17). The Scriptures affirm that God has *given* believers in Jesus his Holy Spirit. Baptism in the Spirit is not something to be earned or a special reward. It is the gift of God.

GIVER OF POWER

? 9. According to 1 John 3:24 how do we know that God is living in us? (Compare Romans 5:5 and 8:9 as well as 1. Thessalonians 4:8.)

What is a "baptism"?

The expression "baptism" is used in various ways in the Bible. It refers, of course, to the water rite, which initiates a person publicly into the church. But the Apostle Paul also describes, for instance, Israel's crossing of the Red Sea as a kind of baptism (1 Corinthians 10:1–2) and John the Baptist spoke of a "baptism in fire" that was an image of the judgment expected to come in the Messianic age (Luke 3:16–17).

In every kind of baptism, though, there are *four parts*: obviously, there is the *agent* that does the baptizing and the *object* of the baptism (the one being baptized). But there is also an *element* or medium in which the baptism takes place. Finally, there is the *purpose* for which the baptism takes place.

It is enlightening to compare, then, the baptism of John with baptism in the Holy Spirit. In the Gospel of John, chapter 1, John the Baptist insists three times that his baptism is *in* or *with* water; water was the *element* of John's baptism. He was, of course, the *agent* doing the baptizing, and Israelites were the *object* of the baptism (Matthew 3:5 specifies Jewish people that came from "Jerusalem and all Judea and all the region near the Jordan River".)

? 10. According to John 1:29–31 what was the *purpose* of the baptism performed by John (especially v. 31)?

Baptism in the Spirit

The expression "baptism (or baptize) in the (Holy) Spirit" is used a total of 7 times in the New Testament. The *first four uses of the expression* are found in the prediction of John the Baptist (Matthew 3:11; Mark 1:8; Luke 3:16; and John 1:33), in which he promised the coming of *another* "Baptizer". When something is repeated in all four

Gospels, that is a clear indication of its importance and that we should pay special attention to what is being said!

11. Identify the *agent* and *element* of the baptism in the Holy Spirit from John 1:33:

agent _____
(who does the baptizing?)

element _____
(in or with what does the baptism take place?)

The *fifth and sixth uses* of the expression are in the book of Acts: the Risen Jesus quoted John's prophecy in Acts 1:5 ("in a few days you will be baptized in the Holy Spirit") and Peter applied the same prophecy to the events surrounding the conversion of the first Gentiles (Acts 11:16).

The only other occurrence of the expression in the New Testament is found in 1 Corinthians 12:12–13. There the Apostle Paul writes: "12 For just as the body is one and has many members, and all the members of the body, though many, are one body, so it is with Christ. 13 For in *one* Spirit we were all baptized into *one* body—Jews or Greeks, slaves or free—and all were made to drink of *one* Spirit."

In Verse 13 of 1 Corinthians 12, the word "one" is repeated *3 times* for emphasis: "one Spirit" (2 x) and "one body".

12. Note the other emphasis in v. 13:

"We were _____ baptized into *one* body—Jews or Greeks,

slaves or free—and _____ were made to drink of *one* Spirit."

We now have enough data to reflect for a moment on the four parts of the baptism in the Holy Spirit.

Agent : Jesus (he does the baptizing)

Element : The Holy Spirit (the "in" or "with" or "through" which the baptism takes place).

Object : "we all" (all believers)

Purpose : "into one body" (incorporation into the body of Christ)

In 1 Corinthians 12–14, the Apostle Paul discusses the *diversity* of the gifts of the Holy Spirit (we will study the gifts of the Spirit in Chapter 9), but he emphasizes first and foremost the *unity* that comes from the Holy Spirit. Verse 13 of 1 Corinthians 12 is the keystone of this unity: the baptism in the Holy Spirit is what creates the body of Christ. It is the great uniting experience of *all* who belong to him. We *all* share in this baptism and "drink" of the same Holy Spirit. Thus, "to be baptized in the Holy Spirit" and "to be given the Holy Spirit to drink" are equivalent expressions. All believers have this in common.

We already saw that the "gift" and the "baptism" of the Spirit are one and the same thing. They describe this same blessing that each and every person who belongs to Christ has received – and this implies that it has to be placed at the *beginning* of the Christian experience, since it is a *universal* blessing given to all disciples of Jesus and not just a special experience of some believers.

Thus, the baptism in the Holy Spirit, *as the New Testament uses this expression*, is not something that a true follower of Jesus needs to seek or pray for, but a blessing we should *look back upon* with thankfulness, to the time when God put us in Christ and made us new creatures.

Growth

In 1 Corinthians 6:19 the Apostle Paul writes that our bodies are a "temple of the Holy Spirit" within us.

13. What consequences do you think this should have on the way we live our lives?

14. Are there any areas of your "life in the body" that you would like to see changed in light of this truth?

Wisdom

Some Christians resist the implications of the texts that we just studied. We have seen that, for the New Testament writers, the baptism in the Holy Spirit is an initial experience of all believers

Some, however, want to teach that baptism in the Spirit is something *subsequent* to coming to faith and finding new life in Christ. They try to get around the clear statement in 1 Corinthians 12:13 that "we were *all* baptized with one Spirit into one body" by arguing that this refers to a *different* baptism. "Yes," they admit, "the Spirit baptism in 1 Corinthians 12:13 is part of the experience of all believers." "But," they continue, "that is not the same baptism as that referred to in the other six passages where the expression 'baptism (or baptize) in the Spirit' is used." They claim that 1 Corinthians 12:13 is a baptism by the Holy Spirit (as agent) into the body of Christ. However, such a position involves some major errors in interpretation.

First of all, an important principle of biblical interpretation is that texts in the Bible should be used to help interpret each other. We saw in this chapter that the expression "baptism (or baptize) in the Spirit" is used a total of 7 times in the New Testament. In *six* of these, the expression unquestionably refers to a work of *Jesus* as the "baptizer", giving us the gift of the Holy Spirit and incorporating us into his body, his people.

1 Corinthians 12:13 would thus be the *only* place in Scripture where the Spirit would be the *agent* of the baptism. In all other instances, Christ is clearly the agent doing the baptism and the Spirit is the element or sphere in which we are baptized. But the expression in the original Greek text is exactly the same in all seven instances. Thus, the natural interpretation of the expression in 1 Corinthians 12 demands understanding "baptism in the Spirit" in the same way as in the other texts. This natural interpretation should be followed unless there were persuasive arguments against it. But there is *not* a good argument against interpreting all seven uses of the expression as referring to one and the same experience. In fact, whenever the verb "baptize" is used in the New Testament about *any* baptism, the Greek preposition

en ("with" or "in") always expresses the *element* of the baptism, not its *agent*.

Finally, if 1 Corinthians 12:13 were different from all the other texts and the Holy Spirit were the *agent* (the *baptizer*) there would be no *element* for the baptism. With what would the Spirit then baptize us?

Principles of sound interpretation and simple logic demand that we understand all seven New Testament uses of the expression "baptism (or baptize) in the Spirit" to be referring to the same work *of Jesus* in which he baptizes all who truly come to faith in him in the Spirit. He "gifts" them with his Spirit and by this act incorporates them into his living body, with all the privileges and responsibilities that this brings with it.

Chapter 6
The Filling of
the Holy Spirit

Orientation

The baptism in the Holy Spirit is the work of Jesus that incorporates a believer into the spiritual reality of his body. As the letter to Titus puts it:

> "He saved us, not because of works done by us in righteousness, but according to his own mercy, by the washing of regeneration and renewal of the Holy Spirit, whom he poured out on us richly through Jesus Christ our Savior." (Titus 3:5–6)

Indeed, the baptism in the Spirit is the hallmark that Christ stamps upon each person who truly is his. The Christian life begins with the reception of the Spirit. As the Apostle Paul says, "Anyone who does not have the Spirit of Christ does not belong to him". (Romans 8:9) Paul had made this crystal-clear in his letter to the Galatians. The gift of the Spirit makes us children of God and puts us "in Christ". To become a genuine Christian means, therefore, receiving the Holy Spirit. And Paul explains that faith alone is the key (on the human side of things) to receiving the promised Spirit; and this faith is stirred up by hearing the message of Christ (Galatians 3:1–5; 3:14).

But what about the thousands of followers of Jesus throughout history from many cultures who have testified to a definite and profound *post*-conversion experience of God's Holy Spirit in which they were shaken out of their complacency or equipped in a new way for service for God? The Scripture makes clear that all genuine believers have received the Holy Spirit – he *lives* in them; they have been *baptized* in him; he will not leave a believer in Jesus. However, even though all true Christians are *indwelt* by the Holy Spirit, it is possible for

Christians to live without experiencing the *power* of the Spirit in their lives – to live a lifestyle that lacks his dynamic. These believers are "pilot light" Christians: the Holy Spirit indwells them much like the pilot light in a furnace that has not been turned up to full force; but he does not fill (empower) them with all the power actually available to every Christian to live an abundant, fruitful life in Christ.

Each and every follower of Jesus needs the power of the Spirit for life and service. It is not possible to really live the Christian life in our own strength. We need to be continually *filled* (empowered) with God's Spirit. While the *baptism* in the Spirit is a unique event incorporating each believer into Christ (it happens only once at the beginning of the spiritual life of each believer), the *filling* of the Spirit must be appropriated by faith moment-by-moment. The filling of the Spirit occurs many times. The filling of the Spirit, i.e., the power of the Holy Spirit in our lives, can be lost (due to sin in our lives, which short-circuits the Spirit's power in us); this power can also be recovered. It seems clear, as well, that the Holy Spirit can fill each individual Christian *more* or *less*. There are degrees of joy, blessing and spiritual power.

Connection

On the day of Pentecost Jesus "poured out" the Spirit of God on his people and baptized in the Spirit the small band of apostles and other disciples and then 3,000 others who were converted through Peter's preaching. Jesus did the baptizing, pouring out the Spirit on them.

1. What was the result among the first group (Acts 2:3–4)?

v. 3: _____

v. 4: they were all _____

and began to _____

Not every group or individual described in the book of Acts that believed in Christ experienced the same outward signs as this first group when they believed and were baptized in the Spirit. Scripture does not teach that "speaking in tongues" (even in the form of a "prayer language") is an indispensable sign of having received the Spirit. There is no record of the 3,000 who were converted later on the day of Pentecost speaking in tongues, for instance. Actually, only three groups in the book of Acts are said to have "spoken in tongues": the small group on Pentecost in Jerusalem; the converts in the home of Cornelius the Centurion at the "Gentile Pentecost" in the coastal town of Caesarea; and the followers of John the Baptist in Acts 19. The first believers went out and proclaimed the Risen Christ. They called men and women to repent and believe in Jesus. There is no record of them ever challenging people to be "baptized in the Spirit".

But, without the inspiration and empowering of the Spirit, the early followers of Jesus could never have borne such effective witness to the Risen Lord.

2. How does Acts 4:31 describe the result of believers being filled with the Holy Spirit?

3. How did this affect their relationships with one another (Acts 4:32–35)?

Exploration

The Spirit of Jesus

For Luke, Jesus is the model and paradigm of what it means to be "Spirit-filled." The Holy Spirit descended upon Jesus at his baptism to anoint and equip him for his ministry as Messiah (*Messiah* means "anointed one"!).

Jesus claimed that the description of the Anointed One in Isaiah applied to him. After reading the Scripture in a synagogue service, he announced that the prophetic passage from Isaiah he had just read pointed to him:

> "The Spirit of the Lord is upon me, because he has anointed me to proclaim good news to the poor. He has sent me to proclaim liberty to the captives and recovering of sight to the blind, to set at liberty those who are oppressed, to proclaim the year of the Lord's favor." (Luke 4:18–19)

4. How does Luke describe Jesus' further experience of the Spirit at the beginning of his public ministry?

Luke 4:1 _____

Luke 4:14 _____

For the Apostle Paul, any true experience of the Holy Spirit is also inseparably tied to Jesus: he is the source and content of any geniune encounter with God. The Spirit of God is, for Paul, the "Spirit of Christ". *The Apostle viewed the believer's experience of Christ and the experience of the Spirit as the same reality.* In Romans 8:9–11 he uses a series of phrases to describe the same fundamental experience of the believer: "the Spirit of God lives in you" = "having the Spirit of Christ" = "Christ is in you".

The hallmark of the Christian life is the experience of the Spirit as an experience of the living Christ. To be "spiritual" means, for Paul, to be in the process of being transformed by the Spirit more and more into the exact likeness to Jesus – to have the characteristics of Christ's life increasingly reproduced in us (Romans 8:26–29; 2 Corinthians 3:18). Paul also makes clear that one cannot truly experience Christ apart from the Spirit.

"Be filled with the Spirit"

The clearest text in the Scriptures in regard to the filling of the Holy Spirit is in Ephesians 5:18–21. It is always helpful, though, to take a look at the broader context in which a passage like this is found. The Apostle makes clear from the beginning of the Book of Ephesians that he is writing to people who have already received God's Spirit.

CHAPTER 6: THE FILLING OF THE SPIRIT

? 5. According to Ephesians 1:13–14, what relationship did the Holy Spirit already have to these believers?

? 6. When did this take place (v. 13)?

Although these believers had already been "sealed with the Spirit" (= they were "baptized in the Spirit" = they *had received* the gift of the Spirit), Paul urged them to seek a deeper *filling* with the Holy Spirit.

? 7. What can happen in our relationship with the Holy Spirit according to Ephesians 4:30?

Yet, this is obviously not the way things are meant to be in the life of the believer in Jesus.

? 8. What two commands are given us in Ephesians 5:18?

Negative ("do not") _____

Positive ("but") _____

First, let's look at the *negative* command. The early church was not full of quiet little people from pious backgrounds. There were plenty of former pagans freshly converted out of raw heathenism into the light of the Gospel. Paul described a situation in the harbor town of Corinth (1 Corinthians 11:20–22) where church suppers and Communion could easily turn into drunken partying! Perhaps a similar danger prompted him to draw the line in Ephesus.

The *positive* command in Ephesians 5:18 is not just an "ideal" or a recommendation, but a *command* (it is in the "imperative" or "command" form in Greek). One of the characteristics of a command of God which he directs toward us is that God wants the recipient to obey it. This implies that God *commands* and *expects* us to be filled with the Holy Spirit.

But the command is not to "fill yourself" with the Spirit, but to "*be filled*"; i.e., to let *God* fill us with the Spirit. Being filled with the Spirit is definitely not the product of self-effort. What God wants is not our self effort and ability, but our *availability* to him. "Be filled…" is a single word in the original Greek text and this word controls everything that follows after it. It is the "peg" on which all the following verses hang.

? 9. What are the results when we are filled with the Spirit, according to Ephesians 5:19–21?

? 10. List the objective results of being filled with the Holy Spirit, which are:

Results in our relationship with God *Results in our relationship with other people*

Growth

In Ephesians 5:1–2 the Apostle Paul explains that the our lives should be motivated by our direct experience of God's love:

"Therefore be imitators of God, as beloved children. And walk in love, as Christ loved us and gave himself up for us, a fragrant offering and sacrifice to God."

When we read the New Testament, though, we quickly become aware of the failure of many Christians today to live on this "normal" level of spiritual life that the Bible envisions for people who know Christ, who are children of God.

However, such sub-level Christian life is *not* evidence that these believers need to be *baptized* in the Spirit – if they belong to Christ at all, then he has already poured out his Spirit upon them. Rather, the sub-normal Christian living that is found among many groups today is evidence of the need to be *filled* with the Spirit. The baptism in the Holy Spirit is not the same as the filling of the Holy Spirit! God, through his Spirit, "has rescued us from the dominion of darkness and brought us into the kingdom of his beloved Son" (Colossians 1:13). When that happened, a new relationship was created between God and us. However, for the rest of our lives this relationship will remain in need of renewal. It is actually possible to "sadden" the Spirit of God through disobedience and choosing to live for self. Whenever sin and unbelief short-circuit our relationship with God our fellowship with him is blocked – then our rapport with him needs to be restored.

"How can I be filled with the Holy Spirit?"

The crucial question: Is there any shadow of sin in my life that stands between God and me? In this chapter we learned that it is possible to *grieve* the Holy Spirit.

11. Read Ephesians 4:25–32 and list the *actions* and *attitudes* mentioned in this passage that can grieve the Spirit.

12. Are any of these a particular temptation or challenge to you personally?

Everything that disturbs our relationship with God needs to be opened up to him and admitted as sin (more on that in the next chapter). Honesty about oneself is the first step.

Ephesians 5:18 demonstrates that being filled with the Holy Spirit is not attainable through our own efforts. The key to living a fruitful, Spirit-filled Christian life is not our own strength or natural gifting, but rather our openness and availability to God.

When it comes to being filled with the Spirit, every attempt to do it on our own is out of the question – it has nothing to do with our own work. This means that only one alternative remains: the filling of the Holy Spirit is something that *God* does out of unconditional love toward us; it is an *act of God's grace*.

Such an act of God is what Paul describes in the same letter as the primary, foundational and essential experience of being a Christian:

> "For by grace you have been saved through faith. And this is not your own doing; it is the gift of God, not a result of works, so that no one may boast." (Ephesians 2:8–9)

Consequently, *God's* work in us is characterized by the following basic pattern: *by* grace (i.e., the dynamic does not originate from our own resources), through *faith* (i.e., the foundation is not our own performance, but rather something we receive as a gift). There is the *giver* (God), the *gift* (in this case being filled and empowered with and by the Holy Spirit) and a *receiver* (the one who trustingly accepts the gift).

Ask God in faith

What, then, do I need to do to be filled with the Holy Spirit? The Holy Spirit of God wants to fill every one of God's people. That is expressed in the command form in Ephesians 5:18. If, however, the filling of the Holy Spirit cannot be accomplished through our own efforts then it remains an unconditional gift of God, which we can only receive thankfully with open, outstretched hands. All we need to do is ask God. He will act when, where and how he wants to.

How the Holy Spirit manifests himself in our lives is up to him. In some cases, it may be something quite visible: the Spirit may give a person the courage to boldly proclaim Christ to the world around them. In other cases, it may be more inconspicuous: the Spirit may give someone a new joy, passion and ability to serve behind the scenes. The Holy Spirit will usually renew and change our lives in harmony and alignment with the basic structure of our personality. God's knowledge of us is perfect and complete – and the Spirit was involved in the original creation of each one of us (Psalm 139:13–16). God's handiwork is always precise! There is no need to be afraid that the Holy Spirit might force or bully us to become something we are not. God's Spirit leads us to our *true* self. All that's expected is our trust and availability.

Wisdom

The writers of the New Testament drew from a rich treasure of symbols and concepts, above all in the Hebrew Bible, that they could use to explain spiritual experience. As a result, they would often use several different metaphors to describe one and the same spiritual reality. When one is studying the Bible, it is important to keep this fact in mind. For instance, what Luke described as "the gift of the Spirit" was also called by him and the Apostle Paul the "baptism in the Spirit". In addition, Paul wrote of the "sealing of the Spirit" (Ephesians 1:13; 4:30). The letters of John seem to prefer calling this our "anointing" from God (1 John 2:20, 27; see also 2 Corinthians 1:21–22).

It is important not to become confused by this multiple imagery. The "gift" and "baptism" of the Spirit, the "sealing" of the Spirit, the "anointing" of the Spirit, and the "enlightenment" from the Spirit (2 Corinthians 4:4; cf. Hebrews 6:4) all refer to the reality that comes about when a person places their trust in Christ. The Spirit's person and work is the one over-arching reality behind all of these images and metaphors.

Chapter 7
The Flesh
and the Spirit

Orientation

The *filling* of the Holy Spirit is a work of God's Spirit in the life of the believer that becomes *outwardly* visible: the Spirit empowers us for fellowship, service and witness and manifests God's love and creativity through us to the world and to other believers. There is, however, also an *inner* dimension of the work of the Spirit in our life and that is the subject of this chapter: the struggle of faith in our own personal experience.

It is important to recognize that there is not just one "power center" in the life of the believer, but *two*. The *Spirit of God* and the *flesh* are the terms that the Apostle Paul introduced for these two poles. *Either* the Spirit *or* the flesh rules our life, but both are always present – either in the background or the foreground. One or the other power is always expressing itself, i.e., being dominant. Paul describes the manifestations of the Spirit and the flesh with two metaphors: the *works* of the flesh and the *fruit* of the Spirit (Galatians 5:19–25). In this chapter we will examine the nature of the struggle between the Spirit and the flesh; in the next chapter we will look more closely at the fruit of the Spirit.

Connection

In the book of Romans, Chapter 8, the Apostle Paul presents an absolute contrast. In that text, there are only two possible positions: either life with Christ or life estranged from God.

1. How does Paul describe these two possible alternatives (Romans 8:6)?

Yet, even in the context of such a radical contrast, Paul looks briefly at the responsibility of the believer to *live* in a way consistent with our real life in Christ.

2. With "God's Spirit living in us", what is our responsibility according to Romans 8:12–14?

The Apostle Paul writes in the Book of Romans about living "according to the flesh." In this context, *flesh* does not mean the *physical body*, but the entire human personality – living, thinking, willing and deciding – in *self-directedness* rather than *God-directedness*.

Later in the same letter, Paul contrasts the "works of darkness" with the "armor of light" which the believer is urged to put on.

3. According to Romans 13:13, what are these "works of darkness"?

4. What are the positive and negative actions we are to undertake in the struggle between light and darkness in our own lives (Romans 13:14)?

However, there is one question that the book of Romans does not really discuss: What happens if a believer lives in contradiction to his or her true calling as a child of God – if we choose, in other words, to live according to our own self-directed inclinations? For a discussion of that question we need to look at the correspondence of the Apostle Paul with the Corinthians.

Exploration

The Church in the World – the World in the Church

The Greek seaport of **Corinth** was one of the major cities of the Roman Empire and the Apostle Paul spent at least a year there teaching the Gospel and planting a church. The group of people he recruited to the Faith ended up causing him a great deal of heartache. The Corinthians were proud residents of a sophisticated, world-class city. Intelligent and articulate, the new believers were familiar with the ideals and lifestyle of the social and cultural elite that set the tone in the city, although probably few if any of them actually came from the upper echelon. They tended to model their behavior after the sophisticated teachers who resided in or regularly visited their cosmopolitan city and held seminars and classes for the privileged few and those social-climbers who wanted to win a place among the elite.

The society of Corinth was dominated by a ruthless, competitive spirit, exemplified by the fact that it was the first city in Greece to hold Roman gladiatorial contests in which professional fighters would battle wild animals or each other to the death for the entertainment of the crowds.

When groups of young, upper-class Corinthians and social-climbers got together, they would argue over who was the best seminar leader and who of them offered the best assertiveness training. The "gurus" who offered these seminars and courses in Corinth were called *rhetors* (the word "rhetoric" – the art of speech delivery – comes from the same root). *Rhetors* were usually sponsored by wealthy and influential persons. They trained people to take part in lawsuits, disputes and discussions in the groups and civic forums of the city. These meetings were characterized by debate, biting criticism of one's opponent, arrogant boasting, and braggadocio. Perhaps not surprisingly, the Corinthian church was racked by strife and internal division.

Three Types of People

In response to the problems in the Corinthian church, Paul spelled out very clearly the possibility of a believer living a life inconsistent with one's calling as a Christian.

Read 1 Corinthians 2:6–3:4. It is important to remember when studying this text that the Apostle continues to address the Corinthian believers as true Christians. Initially, he spells out two different approaches to life in very sharp terms by contrasting the "wisdom" of the world with the wisdom of God. Earthly rulers who live according to the accepted norms of the world system (v. 6 and 8) exemplify the "wisdom" of the world. These are the kind of people, Paul writes, who completely misjudged Jesus and were blind to the secret purposes of God. In reality, they were fools in God's eyes; they knew nothing of true wisdom, otherwise they would not have crucified the Messiah!

> **?** 5. What makes Christians different from these models of earthly acumen and success (1 Corinthians 2:10, 12)?

The "Natural" Person and the Spiritual Person

> **?** 6. How are these earthly authorities and other "natural people" described in 1 Corinthians 2:14?

The word translated "natural" in most English Bibles comes from the Greek word *psyche* (our modern word "psychology" comes from this same root). For the Greeks, the *psyche* was the dynamic principle of life, perception, and reason. Paul's term in 1 Corinthians, "*psychikos*", means a man or woman who has physical life and natural human capabilities and reason, but without God's Spirit. They only have the "flesh" (*sarx* – see the comments about *sarx* on the next page). These "natural" or "soulish" people use only human intellect, judgment and other capacities to evaluate life and the world around them. They are thus not able to correctly estimate or understand spiritual matters; these things often appear to be foolishness to them. Paul contrasts this "natural" person with the "spiritual person [*pneumatikos*]". (*Pneuma* is, of course, the Greek word for "spirit".) The "spiritual" person does not live by the conventional standards and wisdom of the world.

> 7. According to 1 Corinthians 2:15–16, what characterizes the "spiritual person"?

With his explanation of these two categories of people, Paul would seem at first glance to be at the end of his discussion of the possible approaches and strategies to life one can adopt – either one is living by the standards, values and attitudes of the world (a "natural" or "soulish" person), or one has received God's Spirit and knows and lives out the reality of what God has given us as followers of Jesus (1. Corinthians 2:12). But Paul was not finished with his discussion.

The "Fleshly" (Carnal) Person

Somewhat abruptly, the Apostle refocuses his analysis on the situation among the Corinthian believers. Review briefly 1 Corinthians 3:1–4.

> 8. What was the inconsistent and contradictory condition of the Corinthian Christians (1 Corinthians 3:1)?

CHAPTER 7: THE FLESH AND THE SPIRIT

In spite of the fact that they should have been displaying the maturity of *spiritual* men and women (*pneumatikoi*), the Corinthians tended to continue living with the perspective and value system of their old life. They were not "soulish" or "natural" people (*psychikoi*), because that would mean that they did not have the Holy Spirit. But, at the same time, they were not living as they could and should have as followers of Christ. Their lives were characterized by contradiction: not only contradiction regarding God's purposes and plans for them, but also regarding their true being and calling. Paul calls them "fleshly" or "carnal" (i.e. "flesh-oriented") people (*sarkinoi*).

The term *flesh* (Greek = *sarx*) is used in a number of different ways in the Bible. Paul is the one, however, who introduced the use of the word in contrast to the *Holy Spirit* (although he sometimes also used it in a different, more physical sense). Flesh or *sarx* in the letter to the Corinthians does *not* mean the human body. It is not a *part* of human nature in the sense that the *sarx* would be the outer shell whereby the soul or the human spirit would then be a "superior" inner sphere of our nature. The *flesh* is our entire natural orientation as sinful human beings, i.e. as individuals separated from God by our rebellion against him (Romans 8:7). Our flesh is what every person *is* "without God" – our whole nature in its separation from our Maker and in our rebellion against God's leadership in our lives – disconnected from the source of life originating from the Spirit of God.

Paul was quite aware that the ever-potent power of the flesh is still fully present and very active in the life of a believer. The flesh has not been eradicated. Its hostility toward the will of God and his purpose for us can be "triggered" at any time. This essential nature of our God-alienated humanity still exercises an overwhelming, magnetic power – even over the person who seriously wants to follow Jesus.

? 9. According to Galatians 5:17, what is the state of affairs between the power center of the "flesh" and the Spirit of God in the life of a Christian?

Human nature can be described in accordance with its orientation. In his letter to the Romans Paul writes about two opposite *mindsets*: that of the flesh and that of the Spirit. By "mindset" I mean the basic framework and parameters that we use to orient ourselves and interpret life and the world around us. It is the particular way in which we experience ourselves and the surrounding world and how we understand and integrate that information. According to the Apostle Paul, there exists not only the dynamic of the Spirit in the life of a Christian but also the opposing power of his or her flesh (*sarx*). A Christian can take on the mindset (orientation) of either the Spirit or the flesh.

10. How does Romans 7:18 describe the "dynamic" or "power source" of the flesh?

11. What is the consistent direction in which our "*sarx*" pulls us, according to Romans 7:25?

The *flesh* is fully present in the life of every person, then, including Spirit-filled Christians! It stands in opposition to the Holy Spirit who was given to us by God.

12. According to 1 Corinthians 3:3–4, what attitudes and behavior signalled that the Corinthians were orienting their thinking and behavior according to the "flesh"?

13. How does a "fleshly" believer often view themself according to 1 Corinthians 3:18?

Summary

In the New Testament words such as "natural/soulish", "spiritual", or "fleshly/carnal" have a very definite content and connotation:

The natural or "soulish" person *(psychikos)* is an individual in their "nature", as he or she came into the world, grew up, and developed ways and strategies to cope with their life and environment. Spiritual things do not really fit into this perspective. To her/him the work of God in Christ, in particular, remains a mystery, mere "foolishness" (1 Cor 1:18). This person is missing a spiritual "antenna". There is only one possible mindset for the natural person, that of their *"natural"* life. The "natural" man or woman can be polite, clever, very helpful or even religious; however, the mindset, mentality and values, the attitude, desires and objectives they have are those of human nature apart from God's Life and his Spirit.

The "spiritual" person *(pneumatikos)* has opened his or her heart to the guidance of the Spirit of God and has submitted all of life to the Spirit's authority. This person is indwelt and led by the Spirit of God. That does *not* mean that he or she is perfect or has "arrived"; they are in process, on a journey toward spiritual maturity. This person lives according to guidelines established by God, experiences the leadership of the Holy Spirit in all of life and is increasingly capable of understanding events and people from a spiritual perspective.

The "fleshly" or "carnal" person *(sarkinos)*: For the Christian there is not merely one possible lifestyle with a spiritual mindset. Just as the person without Christ, a Christian can live life according to the old values, according to the flesh *(sarx)*. If a Christian does not orient life according to the mindset, values, guidelines and objectives established by God, but rather in accordance with their old lifestyle and environment, then he or she is a fleshly or "carnal" person.

This carnal person is spiritually immature and not free. A carnal person is driven by their impulses and basic human drives instead of being led by the Spirit of God. Carnal Christians are dependent upon other individuals and groups that surround them. That leads to tension and conflict with oneself and with others. "Jealousy and quarreling" are characteristic of a community made up of such carnal or "fleshly" individuals (1 Corinthians 3:3).

Growth

It is entirely possible for a Christian to behave in opposition to his or her true calling. But this person then becomes *an individual living in contradiction*. James 1:8 speaks of the "two-souled" or double-minded person who is "unstable in all he does". Any Christian who lives life in the mindset of the flesh will be a deeply torn, divided individual.

> 14. Where would you place yourself on the scale of soulish/natural, spiritual or fleshly/carnal? Which of these "snapshots" best describes your own personal situation?

> 15. In Romans 6:11–13 what does Paul say the believer should do in the battle between the "flesh" and the Spirit?

It is very clear in Romans 6:11-13 that "flesh" (*sarx*) does not refer to the body. There is certainly no justification for any "anti-body" rhetoric. On the contrary, the parts of our body should serve as "instruments of righteousness"! Hence, the body is viewed as being good. Those who want to live a life of faith are admonished to offer their bodies in service to God and to treat their bodies as he directs.

Wisdom

It is important to read each individual book of the Scriptures carefully before one attempts to compare and transfer the ideas and concepts it presents to other texts in the Bible.

This is particularly the case *when comparing one writer with another*. Before one tries to compare different authors in the Scriptures, one should first clarify what each individual author means.

Such a procedure is also important *even when comparing the writings of a single author*. The letters of the New Testament were usually written to specific local congregations to address particular questions and problems they were facing. In addition, they were written over a period of time and the same writer may have further developed and refined their thinking or approach from one letter to the next. This is surely the case when we consider Paul's approach to the issues involved in the struggle between "flesh" and "Spirit". In the book of Romans, Paul discusses fundamental issues: he presents a clear dichotomy between *two alternative approaches* to and understandings of life (what we have called "mindsets"). He divides humanity into two great camps: those "in the Spirit" (believers in Jesus) and those "in the flesh" (non-believers). Romans clearly calls for the Christian to throw him or herself into the battle on the side of the Spirit, but does not consider in any detail the issue of the believer who *has the Spirit*, but lives oriented to the *flesh*. In 1 Corinthians, though, Paul had been forced to address just this issue in clear terms. In that letter he described this *third* possibility as a man or woman of the flesh (*sarkikos*), and the non-Christian refers to in Romans as "in the flesh," carried the label "a natural man" in 1 Corinthians.

If one does not initially try to understand the differing approaches of these two letters *on their own* but instead jumps to comparisons without sorting out what each has to say individually, it can lead to tremendous confusion. Hence, a fundamental principle of biblical interpretation is to *try to make sense of what a text is saying on its own before you compare it with parallel passages*.

Chapter 8
Life in
the Spirit

Two questions arise when we begin reflecting on what we have learned up to this point. We have seen how a Christian can choose between a "spiritual" (Spirit-oriented) mindset and a "carnal" or flesh-oriented one. But how can one move "back" from being a carnal person to being a spiritual man or woman? And… how are we to actually live our lives "in the Spirit"?

In this chapter, we will examine what life in the Spirit means from the perspective of Scripture. We will first look again at the relationship between being *filled* with God's Spirit by faith, which is the basis and power source of our walking on God's path and our actual *life in the Spirit*, which calls for our active effort and struggle as we "cooperate" with God.

Then, we will study three of the great New Testament traditions in order to compare how they view the relationship between God and the believer "on the road", as we live for God: the teaching of *the Johannine tradition* on "light and darkness"; the *teaching of Paul* on spiritual transformation; and, finally, the teaching of *the tradition of Peter* on participation in the divine nature.

Connection

Before we look at the texts of these biblical traditions more closely, we should take a moment to think about an issue touching all aspects of life in the Spirit.

It is clear in all the writings of the New Testament that our primary relationship to God cannot be restored by our own performance and effort. Spiritual restoration and "rebirth" is a work of God's pure grace, accepted as a gift by the open, receptive hand of faith. However, this does not imply that the believer is then passive. This is clear from the teaching of Ephesians, chapter 2:8-10: "For by grace you have been saved through faith," it says. "And this is not your own doing; it is the gift of God, not a result of works, so that no one may boast."

We are delivered from our sin by no work of our own. It is God's gracious gift. But this does not mean that no "action" in our lives results. The passage goes on to say: "For we are his workmanship, created in Christ Jesus *for good works*, which God prepared beforehand, *that we should walk in them.*"

It is God's grace that brings us to faith and our ongoing life in the Spirit is lived in the light of this grace and by his power. But "good works" – a changed and transformed relationship to ourselves, those around us, and our world – is the result. Our lives are to reflect the beauty of his character and the skill of his craftsmanship.

1. According to Galatians 2:19–20a how are we identified with Jesus in his death?

Christ's sacrifice opens the way for us to return to God – a way *not* dependent upon the "righteousness" that comes through perfect observance of God's Law (Galatians 2:21). Now, through the gift of Christ, all of life has a new foundation.

But when the Apostle says in Galatians 2:20 he "no longer lives" it does *not* mean that he has become a passive observer to life while God takes over all control and "does everything". In the very same verse, Paul says he *does* live, but on a completely different basis than under the pressure of having to perfectly keep the Law of God (*Torah*).

> 2. According to Galatians 2:20, what is this new foundation for life? (Compare also Paul's comment in Colossians 2:6.)

Life in the Spirit, in fact, calls not for passivity but for our active effort and exertion.

> 3. According to Galatians 5:16, how are those who belong to Christ supposed to find the power to resist the impulses that come from their "flesh" – their life as it was without the Spirit of God? (Compare also Galatians 5:25.)

One of the Apostle Paul's favorite pictures of this dynamic struggle was "putting off" – like an old cloak – our former way of thinking and living and "putting on" the new person we are in Christ. We read in Colossians 3:9–10: "You have put off the old self with its practices and put on the new self."

> 4. What action is the believer to take in order to "put off the old self", according to Colossians 3:5?

> 5. According to Colossians 3:12–14, what are the concrete characteristics of our "new self"?

When we live in the Spirit, God wants our active participation. The Holy Spirit is the one who leads the battle against the flesh (*sarx*) in our life, but we are called upon to actively cooperate in the fight against the drives and pull of our old mindset and lifestyle that would keep us from living for God. He has given us the weapons for this fight; our fathers and mothers of the faith spoke in this context of *aids to faith* or "*media gratiae*" (= channels of grace). These include prayer, the devotional reading and study of Scripture, worship, Communion, and fellowship with other believers, to name a few. We are called upon to actively make use of these aids and tools that God has given to assist us in living a victorious Christian life!

We actively believed in Jesus at our spiritual birth. So, too, we have to actively trust his working in us as we live our daily lives. This is what genuine faith involves.

Exploration

As we turn now to three of the great scriptural metaphors for life in the Spirit, we should keep in mind that we are called upon to actively "keep in step with the Spirit'; to say "Yes!" to his leadership and to take advantage of the means God has provided for *walking* with him.

Light and Darkness

Throughout the Gospel and Epistles of John, life in the Spirit is presented using the metaphor of light and darkness. "God is Light": this is the absolute starting point of all true, biblical spirituality. According to John, there is no "dark side" of God. "In Him is no darkness at all." (1 John 1:5) God's ways are sometimes difficult to understand or even inscrutable, but we can trust that He is good *all* the time and intends only good for us.

6. According to 1 John 1:6, what is inconsistent with saying one has fellowship with God?

? 7. What picture does John use in 1 John 1:7 for life in the Spirit?

In John's writings, then, the key to life with God is *fellowship* with him; that means living day-by-day, hour-by-hour in the light of his presence.

? 8. 1 John 1:9 spells out further what it means to walk with God. What can we do when we allow sin to cause us to stumble or fall?

Spiritual Transformation: The Fruit of the Spirit

In the early chapters of his letter to the Galatians, the Apostle Paul tried to help the Galatians see the danger of losing their liberty in Christ by falling into *legalism* – by trying to live their Christian life on the basis of a set of rules and regulations. But in chapter 5 he addresses a different danger, the danger of misusing one's freedom by living for one's own interests rather than in concern for others. According to Paul, the spiritual person is not the man or woman who uses their liberty to selfishly indulge their own desires. The spiritual person willingly expresses his or her freedom in Christ by serving others. The life of the truly spiritual person exhibits the "fruit of the Spirit" from the heart: "love, joy, peace, patience, kindness, goodness, faithfulness, gentleness, self-control." (Galatians 5:22–23) This is in total contrast with the "works" of the flesh (v. 19).

True Spiritual Freedom

Paul also addressed the issue of spiritual liberty in his Second Letter to the Corinthians. There he writes, "The Lord is the Spirit, and where the Spirit of the Lord is, there is freedom" (2 Corinthians 3:17). The Apostle goes on in the same passage to pick up a metaphor that he had introduced earlier: when Moses communed with God during the

Exodus of Israel from Egypt and the wanderings in the wilderness, the Scriptures report that his face would shine with a reflection of God's glory (Exodus 34:34–35). Afterward, Moses would put a veil over his face. Paul goes on to contrast that situation with life in the Spirit. Those who know Christ are all privileged to have direct access to the divine presence (not just a select representative like Moses); we all behold the glory of God in the person of Jesus (2 Corinthians 4:4–6). Thus, each and every man or woman who knows Christ can experience God's presence directly in the Spirit.

> **?** 9. What impact should this immediate and direct communion with God have on our life (2 Corinthians 3:18)?

Participation in the Divine Nature

The Apostle Paul's metaphor in 2 Corinthians 3 pictures the believer being *transformed* – beginning to "shine" and reflect God's nature – through the light of fellowship with God in Christ.

The Epistle of Second Peter expresses a similar thought with different images. (2 Peter 1:3–11).

> **?** 10. Through knowing God in Christ (2 Peter 1:3), we receive God's promises. What bond does this create between God and us according to 2 Peter 1:4?

"Participation in the divine nature" is a startling idea! Does this mean that we become "divine" and are absorbed as a part of God?

Ancient teachers of the faith used a beautiful picture to explain what is really involved in this process of "sharing in the divine nature": if a piece of iron is held long enough in a blazing fire, the iron begins to absorb the heat – the very "nature" of the fire. It begins to glow with the same color and radiate the same heat as the fire itself. The iron does not *turn into* fire, but rather the fire lends or confers to the iron the characteristics and nature of the fire. In a similar way, 2 Peter 1:4 pictures the transformation of our lives by "participation" in the divine nature. This does not mean that we become "absorbed" into God and disappear (as in some Eastern religions), but that we ourselves are continually transformed through his presence in order that we become more and more like Him.

11. What are *we* to undertake in response to this amazing work of God in our lives (2 Peter 1:5ff)?

Growth

It is very important to intellectually understand the work of the Triune God in our lives. But it is immeasurably more important to *experience* fellowship with God himself. "My soul thirsts for God," the Psalmist sings, "for the living God." (Psalm 42:2) But sometimes it is really difficult for us to recognize just what our soul is trying to tell us! Deep in the innermost chamber of every person lies a secret kept in a tightly locked strongbox. This secret strikes such fear in our hearts that we are willing to do almost anything in order *not* to open the lid. This secret fear, which we surpress or sublimate at all costs, says: "There is nobody… nothing… that can satisfy my deepest desire and needs – I am truly alone!" In order *not* to plunge headlong into deep anger, resentment and possibly depression we need to face up to this fear by allowing God to put his arms around us and to sense him saying: "It's all right, my child, I'm with you! You are valuable and loved!"

12. What is the state of your personal fellowship with God? Do you experience life in the Spirit at the level the Scriptures promise is possible for God's children?

Wisdom

The Psalms compare our longing for God to that of a wild stag that is winded from running and panting for water: "As a deer pants for flowing streams, so pants my soul for you, O God." (Psalm 42:1)

Scripture uses different metaphors to present this one overwhelming reality: we mere human beings can have intimate fellowship with the God of the universe. This is the heart of what true spirituality is really all about: living in the Spirit means living in communion with God himself, in the light of His presence.

To do *theology* or to study the Bible means (in the best case) to reflect on God, his Word and his ways. However, to think about God, as important as that is, can never replace the deep, mysterious, personal encounter with God himself. If we really do theology, if we really study and meditate on the Scriptures, it should lead us to silence and awe before the throne of God. Conversely, it is also true that real fellowship with God leads to cleansed and ordered thinking about him. To think or theologize about God without personally encountering Him at a deeper, almost inexpressible level, would be like attending a class on the "Theory of Swimming" without ever getting into the water! To know God personally and to glorify and enjoy him forever – this is the deepest reason for and the actual objective of Bible study and all true "theology".

"Ὁ θεὸς φῶς ἐστιν καὶ σκοτία ἐν αὐτῷ οὐκ ἔστιν οὐδεμία. 6ἐὰν εἴπωμεν ὅτι κοινωνίαν ἔχομεν μετ' αὐτοῦ καὶ ἐν τῷ σκότει περιπατῶμεν, ψευδόμεθα καὶ οὐ ποιοῦμεν τὴν ἀλήθειαν·"

Ιωαννου Επιστολη Πρωτη 1:5-6

"God is light, and in him is no darkness at all. If we say we have fellowship with him while we walk in darkness, we lie and do not practice the truth."

1. John 1:5-6

GIVER OF GIFTS

The Holy Spirit
and the Church

Chapter 9
The Gifts
of the Spirit

Orientation

In our study so far, we have concentrated upon the work of the Spirit in the individual believer. But not just individuals were impacted by the coming of the Holy Spirit. A new age began for the People of God as well. With this chapter we start the final section of our study of the teaching of the Scriptures about the Holy Spirit: "The Holy Spirit and the Church".

Beginning early in our study, we saw Israel's long-awaited hope that a new age of the Spirit would someday dawn, when the ancient hope of Moses would be fulfilled and *all* the Lord's people would prophesy – that God would pour out his Spirit upon them.

The flame of this hope never died in Israel and it lived on in Jewish tradition. Deuteronomy 34:9 says that "Joshua the son of Nun was full of the spirit of wisdom, for Moses had laid his hands on him". There is a very old commentary-tradition among the rabbis on this Scripture:

> "Rabbi Tanhuma, son of Rabbi Abba (said): The Holy One, blessed be He, said: 'In this world only a few individuals have prophesied but in the World to Come all Israel will be made prophets'; as it says, *'And it shall come to pass afterward, that I will pour out My Spirit upon all flesh; and your sons and your daughters shall prophesy'* (Joel II:28)." (*Num. Rabbah* XV:25 – commenting on Numbers 11:17)

The Apostle Peter announced on Pentecost that this time had truly come in Jesus, that the gift of the Spirit had been poured out upon the people of God (Acts 2:16–17).

The reality that there is "One Body", the body of Christ, is based upon the fact that Christ has baptized each and every one who belongs to him in the Holy Spirit. All of us, the Apostle Paul told the Corinthian believers, belong to that Body by virtue of the fact that all of us were baptized into it through Jesus pouring out his Spirit upon us. (1 Corinthians 12:12–13)

Connection

The gift of God's Spirit creates One Body – one People of God, but this unity is not based upon *uniformity*. The Holy Spirit himself, the basis of our *unity* in Christ, is also the source of the *diversity* of the church. The word in Greek for "spiritual gifts" (Greek: *charismata*) is related to the term for "grace" (*charis*). Thus, these are God's gracious gifts to his people.

Through his gifts of grace (the *charismata*) the Spirit creates a body made up of many different members, with many different functions. There are four passages in the New Testament that discuss the *charismata*. The longest and most famous of these is in the letter of 1 Corinthians 12–14. Other important passages are Romans 12:3–8 and Ephesians 4:7–14; there is also a passing reference to spiritual gifts in 1 Peter 4:10–11. We will concentrate in this chapter almost exclusively on the text in 1 Corinthians.

Before we look closer at 1 Corinthians, though, it is worth noting that all four of the New Testament passages in which spiritual gifts are listed contain a direct statement that *every Christia*n has at least one spiritual gift: Romans 12:3–6; 1 Corinthians 12:11; Ephesians 4:7; and 1 Peter 4:10.

The Apostle Paul particularly emphasized that the *charismata* are manifestations of one and the same Spirit. He also made clear that they are distributed to each and every person who knows Christ. No one is without a gift. "All these are empowered by one and the same Spirit, who apportions to each one individually as he wills." (1 Corinthians 12:11)

1. According to 1 Corinthians 12:7, why is each believer given some manifestation of the Spirit?

Exploration

A comprehensive discussion of all the gifts that are mentioned in the various texts of the New Testament would extend beyond the boundaries of this study. So, we will limit our discussion of the spiritual gifts (*charismata*) to 1 Corinthians 12–14. In this passage clear guidelines are given regarding the use of spiritual gifts based on the example of the gifts of prophecy and speaking in tongues.

We saw in Chapter 7 that the Corinthian church was torn with problems and conflict. These difficulties included partisan attachment to favorite Christian teachers. Intense rivalries grew out of these conflicting loyalties. In addition, the Corinthian believers – especially the wealthy and the social climbers among them – continued to hold tightly to the values of the surrounding culture. They took fellow Christians to court and discriminated against poorer church members when the congregation met in homes belonging to more prosperous believers for fellowship meals, worship and the Lord's Supper. Some of them continued to visit pagan temples, where the best restaurants in the city were to be found and much of the business life of Corinth was carried on.

Some church members were using their more dramatic spiritual gifts – such as "speaking in tongues" – in ways that did not build up the fellowship.

There were disagreements over ethics, particularly about what sexual behavior is appropriate for Christians, both inside and outside marriage. Last, not least, there were major divisions in the church over theological issues such as the resurrection of the body.

Paul sought to address these problems and the attitudes that lay behind them by holding up a "counter-cultural" model for the believers.

Paul called upon them to work together, serving each other in humility. Such humble service, he said, is not the sign of a narrow, uneducated, unsophisticated mentality. Rather, it is part of what it means to truly follow Christ.

> **?** 2. According to Paul, how was Christ himself a model for us of self-sacrificing love (2 Corinthians 8:9)?

One Body – Many Members

We looked at Paul's teaching in 1 Corinthians 12 on baptism in the Spirit in some detail in Chapter 5. The fact that *all* believers in Jesus have been baptized in the Spirit is the bedrock reality that is the foundation of the *body* metaphor that Paul uses to explain and illustrate the unity and diversity of the church. The "members" of the Body are all of the believers, each one gifted with his or her own *charisma* (spiritual gift) (1 Corinthians 12: 27–31).

> **?** 3. Since *all* believers are members of one Body, what does this imply for our relationship to each other (1 Corinthians 12:26)?

No Christian should think in individualistic terms of the importance of "*my*" spiritual gift but remember his or her need for and relation with other members of the Body. There can be no room for spiritual pride and self-aggrandizement, no place for an unbalanced stress on any select gifts.

We saw in Chapter 6 that "speaking in tongues" is not a necessary accompaniment of either the baptism or the fullness of the Spirit. This is confirmed by the form of the questions with which Paul concludes his discussion of the members of the Body and their gifts in 1 Corinthians 12. The Greek language used indicates that he expected a *negative* answer to each of his concluding rhetorical questions:

"Are all apostles? [*No!*] Are all prophets? [*No!*] Are all teachers?
[*No!*] Do all work miracles? [*No!*] Do all have gifts of healing? [*No!*]
Do all speak in tongues? [*No!*] Do all interpret? [*No!*]"

(1 Corinthians 12:29–30)

At first glance, there seems to be a problem here. We have seen that
the prediction of Joel was that *all* of God's people would "prophesy".
Yet in 1 Corinthians 12:29, Paul seems at first glance to be denying
that all believers do so! The answer to this puzzle can found by a
careful examination of exactly what Paul was saying. His *question*
(which expected a negative answer) was *not*: "Do all prophesy?"
(which would carry an implied "No!" answer); the actual question he
posed was: "*Are* all Prophets? [*No!*]" What Paul is denying here is that
all have the *office* or responsibility of a prophet (see v. 12:5). This is
not the case, he says. The question can best be translated, "All are not
prophets, are they?" This does not deny the fact that all Spirit-filled
Christians, at least on occasion, do in fact, prophesy.

It is significant that Paul changes the way he formulates the question
when he comes to tongue-speaking. He does not ask: "Are all tongues-
speakers? [*No!*]" but "Do all speak in tongues? [*No!*]". There is no
office of "tongues-speaker" in Scripture. The question in this case,
since it demands a negative answer, could best be translated: "All do
not speak in tongues, do they?"

The Most Excellent Way

Paul transitions immediately from discussing the diversity of gifts
among the members of the church to his famous chapter on love,
1 Corinthians 13. It is no accident that the Apostle puts this "hymn to
love" at exactly this place. He calls love "the most excellent way".

The image of the *way* comes from the "wisdom" literature of the
Hebrew Bible; for instance, Proverbs 1–3. 1 Corinthians 13 pictures
love as an entire *way of life*. Love transcends each and all of the
spiritual gifts and therefore puts them into their proper perspective.
Love is not one gift among many, but an all-embracing lifestyle that
ought to characterize *every* believer in Jesus, regardless of his or her
specific spiritual gift.

? 4. According to 1 Corinthians 13:1–3, what is the value of even the most dramatic *charismata* apart from love?

Only love validates any particular spiritual gift. Paul contends that even such powerful gifts as prophecy, knowledge and dramatic faith are not just worthless without love, but that exercising them apart from love means that one is a spiritual "zero" – if I "have not love, I am nothing!" (1 Corinthians 13:2). Whatever our different spiritual gifts may be, love is the one central, essential, and irreplaceable sign of the presence of God's Spirit in our lives. The greatest evidence that the new age of the Spirit has dawned, that Messiah has come and has poured out his Spirit upon us, his people, is not the presence of spectacular spiritual manifestations, but the reality of Christ-like love.

The Spirit of Prophecy

? 5. In Peter's speech on the day of Pentecost (Acts 2:16–18), he quotes a prediction of Joel. What are the two phrases that are repeated in this quotation for special emphasis?

"I (God) will _____" (v. 17/v. 18)

"(they) will _____" (v. 17/v. 18)

What is prophecy?

"Prophecy" then, is a mark of the presence of God's Spirit. What is prophecy in the Scriptures, though? The term "prophecy" is extremely broad and used for many different things. In the context of the spiritual gifts it is perhaps best to look directly at what Paul teaches about prophecy in the Corinthian letter.

Paul discusses prophecy in the church in 1 Corinthians 14:29–33. He first states there that *prophecy* implies that something has been *revealed* to a Christian by God. If there is no revelation from God, then there is no prophecy (1 Corinthians 14:30). Second, it seems that prophecy must include a disclosure to other believers – the recipient of the revelation does not keep it private, because all of the gifts of God are for the common good (1 Corinthians 14: 24–26).

> 6. According to 1 Corinthians 14:4, what *purpose* does prophecy have in the church?

If we think about this for a moment, though, a question arises: What is the *authority* of such revelations and proclamations made under the inspiration of the Spirit?

Apostles and Prophets

In the Hebrew Bible, the major prophets (those who stood in the tradition of Moses) seemed to stand apart from the "disciples of the prophets" who gathered in the "schools" of the prophets and also seemed to have prophetic gifts (see, for instance, 1 Samuel 10:6ff; 19:20ff; 2 Kings 2:3, 5, 7, 15–18; 4:38–41). The *Torah* (Five Books of Moses) also makes a distinction between the authority of Moses and that of the "prophets" in the camp of Israel who also were inspired by the Spirit of God (Numbers 11:29; 12:6–8). This can be seen in the transfer of authority from Moses to Joshua: "Joshua the son of Nun was full of the spirit of wisdom, for Moses had laid his hands on him". (Deuteronomy 34:9) The deliberate placing of the hands on someone was understood in Jewish thinking as the ordination – the "setting apart" – of a person for the duties and responsibility of a prophet or other "office bearer". The authority of the one thus set apart was derived from the one laying hands upon them. Jewish tradition preserved this understanding. The rabbis said, for instance:

> "So people were praising Joshua for giving the whole of Israel to drink of his wisdom, but he said: 'Praise ye Moses, who is my source and wisdom," as it says, 'For Moses had laid hands upon him'." (*Exodus Rabbah* XXXI:3 – commenting on Exodus 22:24)

Thus, just because a prophecy was based upon a revelation from God, this did *not* imply that it necessarily had absolute divine authority on the same level as that of Moses. Only Moses and the later prophets who were seen to line up with him had such direct and unquestioned authority.

In the tradition of the Hebrew Bible, a Mosaic-type prophet was to be tested and approved (Deuteronomy 18:14–22). If a prophet claimed to be speaking for God in the sense of Mosaic authority and spoke one false prediction, he was judged to have spoken "presumptuously/ audaciously" – his word was not from the Lord. The penalty for such a transgression was death! But once a prophet was acknowledged as true, the people of God were obliged to obey him. To disobey the authoritative declaration of such a prophet would be to disobey God! His word was not to be trifled with.

> 7. What should *always* take place in the case of New Testament prophecies? (1 Corinthians 14:29; 1 Thessalonians 5:19– 21)?

The command to "test" and "approve" a prophecy suggests that such a prophecy needs to be sifted or evaluated. The Hebrew Bible calls for evaluation of the *prophet*; the Pauline procedure is to evaluate the *prophecy*. This implies that a New Testament prophetic oracle can be *mixed* in quality; the wheat must be separated from the chaff.

An example of such an evaluation of a prophetic word is reported in Acts 21:4, where certain disciples in the city of Tyre urged Paul "through the Spirit" (i.e. in a prophecy – see Acts 11:28), "not to go on to Jerusalem". But Paul chose not to obey this prophetic word; he went up to Jerusalem anyway. There is no indication at all that he ever considered his action to have been a mistake or in some way disobedient to God. Paul seems to have evaluated and rejected the implications of the prophecy. (Even though subsequent prophetic words accurately predicted the result of his journey up to Jerusalem.)

Compared to these prophetic oracles, though, the authority of the *Apostles* was on a different level altogether.

8. How does Paul rate the authority of these kind of prophetic oracles in comparison to his own authority as an Apostle (1 Corinthians 14:37–38)?

For Paul, the *Apostles* (in the narrow sense of the word = those who were the appointed and authorized witnesses of the resurrected Jesus) are the true successors to the authority of Moses, Isaiah and the other prophets whose words are part of Scripture in the Hebrew Bible. The teaching of the Apostles must logically form, then, the basis for the evaluation of prophecy and teaching of any kind. Any prophetic word must agree with the apostolic message or it is to be rejected (1 Corinthians 14:38). Paul's claim to authority is really quite remarkable: "…what I am writing to you is the Lord's command!"

Speaking in Tongues

We have already seen that there were certain members of the church in Corinth that were abusing the gift of tongues. In 1 Corinthians 14, Paul sets out some guidelines for this gift. Before we look at his rules for the use of tongues in the church, though, we should understand a bit more about its function in general. As far as the book of Acts is concerned, the miracle of tongues on the day of Pentecost was clearly an example of the disciples speaking in *intelligible* languages. The kind of speaking in tongues in 1 Corinthians seems to be somewhat different.

9. According to 1 Corinthians 14:2, to whom is a person speaking when they speak in tongues?

10. What kind of use for tongues is implied in 1 Corinthians 14:14 and 14:16?

The Apostle had already made clear (1 Corinthians 12:30) that not all believers speak in tongues. Here, then, he acknowledges that speaking in tongues is a valid form of private prayer and praise (see 14:19); but he sets some limitations to its use in the congregation.

First of all, he says, "one who speaks in a tongue builds up himself", and then goes on to contrast this with the one speaking prophecy, who "builds up the church" (14:4). Paul insists on *intelligibility* in the assembled church, because the growth and encouragement of the Body depends upon it. So, he says, any tongues-speaking in public must be accompanied by interpretation (14:13, 27). Whatever *charisma* is used, everything that is done when the believers meet together must be done for the edification of the church: "All things must be done for building up" the church! (14:26).

Some have tried to use Paul's statement that "one who speaks in a tongue builds up himself" to affirm that tongues-speaking is something for every Christian "because," they argue, "every Christian needs to build him/herself up". This places a wrong emphasis on what the Apostle was saying. The actual framework of what Paul means is that of the *church*: in light of 1 Corinthians 13, to try to build oneself up is much too narrow and small a goal. "Since you are eager for manifestations of the Spirit," he says, "strive to excel in building up the church" (14:12). Paul allows that tongues-speaking without interpretation (and therefore in private) may result in self-edification, but he is certainly not recommending it for this reason.

The second boundary condition for the use of tongues in the church is that it is to be strictly orderly: only one may speak at a time (always with the presupposition that interpretation will follow!) and only two, or at the most three, may speak during a service (14:27–28). There is clear concern on the part of the Apostle that outsiders not be offended by unintelligible and offensive confusion in the church.

The Central Issue

From the teaching of Paul about the *charismata*, in particular about prophecy and tongues, we have been able to focus on the central issues of spiritual gifts:

- Every believer is gifted.
- All gifts are for the building up of the body.
- Each and every gift must be exercised in humble love.

With this in mind, the church must seek appropriate ways to express the life of the Spirit, always being conscious of the impression that is being made on outsiders. The reason for this consideration of the sensibilities of unbelievers is that God himself loves and cares for everyone and we as his people should be careful not to make any unnecessary barriers to their coming to faith.

Growth

1 Corinthians 12–14 make completely clear that spiritual gifts are meant for the good of the Body. Ephesians 4:7–14 emphasizes this from a somewhat different perspective. Where 1 Corinthians primarily focuses on the *gifts* themselves, the Ephesians text focuses on the *gifted believers* who are installed by God into various "offices" or duties in the church. The specific ones mentioned are apostles, prophets, evangelists and pastor-teachers (a combination word).

11. According to Ephesians 4:12 what is the responsibility of these gifted men and women in the church?

It is tragic that this perspective of the real task of these offices has been largely lost in many churches in the Western world. Instead of seeing themselves as "coaches" who help other believers do the work of the ministry, many ministers see themselves as a "one-man band". One wit compared the situation to sports: much of the church, today, he said, is like a basketball game: there are 10 people on the court badly in need of rest and 10,000 people in the stands badly in need of exercise!

CHAPTER 9: THE GIFTS OF THE SPIRIT

12. When you think of your own church, does this sound at all like the situation there? What practical steps do you think you could undertake to help things change for the better?

Wisdom

Our investigation in this chapter touched on one of the most central and important issues in all of religion: the issue of *authority*. Who speaks definitively for God?

The answer of the people of God, beginning with Israel, has been pretty clearly spelled out: the *Prophets* speak for God and, in the New Testament, their successors, the *Apostles*. This is the "deposit of faith" that the generations that followed the Apostles saw themselves called upon to preserve (and to defend when necessary). Timothy, for instance, is exhorted to "guard the good deposit entrusted to you by the Holy Spirit who dwells within us." (2 Timothy 1:14). The little letter of Jude commands believers to "contend for the faith that was once for all delivered to the saints". The teaching of the Apostles is presented as the defense-line of the church against false teaching and its source of certainty in questions of faith and life.

The Apostles are the authoritative teachers of the church. This is also the proper framework for understanding the place of "signs and wonders" – miraculous demonstrations of divine power. The Apostle Paul wrote: "The signs of a true apostle were performed among you [by me] with utmost patience, with signs and wonders and mighty works." (2 Corinthians 12:12) In his letter to the Romans, he spelled out the role of "signs and wonders" even more clearly: "to bring the Gentiles to obedience—by word and deed, by the power of signs and wonders, by the power of the Spirit of God—so that from Jerusalem and all the way around to Illyricum I have fulfilled the ministry of the gospel of Christ." (Romans 15:18–19; see also Hebrews 2:3-4). There is no whiff here of a glorification of "signs and wonders" for their own sake; they are viewed as tools of God for the truly important task of establishing the Gospel among the nations.

"*God did not create the world and then walk away, but rather just as the world comes from him, it also exists in him. Wherever we encounter the truth, he is there! In the innermost part of our hearts he is there; but our hearts have strayed away from him.*"

St. Augustine (Confessions 4,12)

Chapter 10
Discerning
the Spirit

 *Orientation*

We are approaching the end of our journey. Before we finish, though, we need to take a look at the spiritual conflict in which God's people find themselves today. The New Testament speaks of the necessity of "discerning the spirits". Not all spiritual impulses and forces are positive.

The necessity of discerning the source of spiritual impulses and ideas becomes clear when one reads much of what is written today about "spirituality".

Much contemporary teaching about living spiritually or following a transcendent path claims that all spiritual ways are ultimately the same. There exists only one "spirit", one power, in the universe. Everyone participates in it.

Let us take a closer look at this. The idea that everything true has only one source/origin is the firm and unanimous belief of Israel and the Church. In the Gospel of John we read, for example, that the true Light in Jesus "gives light to everyone". (John 1:9) The Holy Spirit is "the Spirit of truth" (John 16:13). St. Augustine reflected on this in his *Confessions*: "God did not create the world and then walk away, but rather just as the world comes from him, it also exists in him. *Wherever we encounter the truth, he is there!* In the innermost part of our hearts he is there; but our hearts have strayed away from him" (*Confessions* 4:12) – or: "My God… *no one apart from you teaches the truth no matter where it may shine.*" (*Confessions* 5:6).

But the assertion that everything true originates from the Spirit of God is something quite different than the claim that there is only *one* spirit and one power that one encounters in all possible expressions of human spirituality.

It is true that everything that exists owes its existence to the creative power of God and is continuously sustained through his power. Israel's songwriters praised God for the fact that he sustains everything that has breath: "When you hide your face," Psalm 104:29–30 says, "they are dismayed; when you take away their breath (*ruach*), they die and return to their dust. When you send forth your Spirit (*ruach*), they are created, and you renew the face of the ground."

Nevertheless, there is an essential difference between this truth and the teaching that all spiritual ways are ultimately the same and that only one "spirit" or spiritual power exists and that everyone on any spiritual path participates in it. In 1 Corinthians 2:12 the Apostle Paul refers to *two* spirits that can both be encountered in spiritual reality: the "spirit of the world" and the Spirit who is from God. The Gospel of John explains that the world is not able to receive the Spirit of truth, "because it neither sees him nor knows him" (John 14:17). Jesus prayed for his people: "Holy Father… keep them from the evil one… Sanctify them in the truth; your word is truth." (John 17:15-17)

Connection

Spiritual manifestations are not necessarily self-interpreting. Their impact and repercussions are always *ambiguous*.

Emotional experiences, bodily effects and religious fervor are not clear indicators that something is definitely the work of God's Spirit. In many different non-biblical and pagan religions people speak in tongues and experience "holy laughter" and ecstatic swooning. Thus, spiritual manifestations in and of themselves prove nothing about their *origin*. Furthermore, any *message* or *content* associated with them, as we have already seen in discussing New Testament prophecy (Chapter 9), must be *tested* on the basis of the teaching of the Prophets and Apostles as they are recorded for us in Scripture. What are the criteria, then, that can help us determine whether or not a spiritual expression or experience is from God's Spirit?

Exploration

The Spirit of God is the Spirit of Jesus

We saw already in Chapter 6 that for the Apostle Paul, Jesus is the source and content of any true encounter with God. The Spirit of God is the "Spirit of Christ" (Romans 8:9; also Galatians 4:6; Philippians 1:19). Any true spiritual experience or spiritual path must directly involve the living Christ or lead toward his Truth and Light. Furthermore, to be "spiritual" means to become more like Christ. Thus, there are two criteria that provide a test for all spiritual claims and experiences, as well as for any manifestation of spiritual gifts: a) *the person and work of Jesus*; and b) *the character of Jesus*.

The Person and Work of Jesus

The two spirits which Paul contrasts in 1 Corinthians 2:12 – the spirit of the world and the Spirit from God – are clearly associated with two different "wisdoms" discussed in 1 Corinthians 1–2: the "wisdom of the world" and the "wisdom of God".

1. According to 1 Corinthians 1:18–24 what is the center point of any spiritual "wisdom" that truly comes from God?

2. What is the *secret of the ages* that Paul was commissioned to proclaim, according to Colossians 1:25–27?

Spiritual enlightenment is not just the recognition of abstract information about the construction or plan of the cosmos or an insight into one's origin, destiny, or spiritual path. Genuine spiritual revelation is a manifestation of the reality of God *in Christ* or leads in the direction of that reality.

GIVER OF GIFTS

At the end of his letter to the Romans, Paul sets out the boundaries for any spiritual revelation or enlightenment.

According to Romans 16:25–27:

? 3. What does any true spiritual revelation have to be "in sync" with? (v. 25)

? 4. What writings does any spiritual revelation have to line up with? (v. 26)

? 5. What result should teaching such spiritual truth have among non-believers? (v. 26)

Because the Spirit of God *is* the Spirit of Jesus, any genuine spiritual experience will be linked with Jesus – focusing on his life, death and resurrection or leading to him and his teaching. This takes place wherever and whenever God manifests and makes himself known through his Spirit. It may still be in the form of an unclear "mystery" for the person who has not yet come to faith, but it must lead toward the Cross. It can be checked by its correspondence with the teaching of the Prophets and the Apostles, as found in the Scriptures.

The Character of Jesus

Since the Spirit of God is the Spirit of Jesus, any true spiritual manifestation or enlightenment will also lead the person or group affected to pattern their own life in a way that is in harmony with the character of Jesus. To be truly "spiritual" is to be like Christ!

CHAPTER 10: DISCERNING THE SPIRIT

In the context of the promise of the Spirit, the prophets of Israel also spelled out this *ethical* dimension of the coming of the Spirit:

> 6. According to Ezekiel 36:26–27 how does the coming of the Spirit impact the *ethical life* of the People of God?

A new inner freedom and a vital personal relationship with God was the hallmark of life in the Spirit for the Apostle Paul. This was the "law of the Spirit" that Paul says sets us free from the "law of sin and death". (Romans 8:2)

> 7. According to Romans 12:2 what does the Christian's capacity for correct ethical decisions depend upon?

Paul attributes the fundamental reshaping and transformation of our inner motivations and moral awareness to the work of the Spirit of God (2 Corinthians 3:3). He describes this in other places as the "mind of Christ".

> 8. According to Colossians 1:9–10, what does true spiritual wisdom and insight result in?

The law of Moses – the *Torah* – still stands for Paul as the standard of righteousness which God expects from us (Romans 8:4), but it is *love* – as exemplified in the life of Jesus – which has become the quintessence of fulfilling the will of God (Romans 13:8–10). Paul writes of being "under the law of Christ" (1 Corinthians 9:21).

To walk in the Spirit and be led by the Spirit means, then, to allow the inner dynamic of God's Spirit to come to concrete expression in our lives through loving word and act – we become more like Jesus. This will always be the direction in which true spiritual enlightenment or true spiritual gifts will lead.

In summary, we can say that the fact that *the Spirit of God is the Spirit of Jesus* leads directly to the conclusion that *Jesus is the true measure* of all possible and various spiritual manifestations. If they are genuinely from God they will lead toward Christ and the result in our lives and our spiritual communities will be the reproduction of Christ-like character in the individual and community. If these characteristics are not present, then the manifestation must be rejected as self-generated or even rooted in spiritual darkness; such manifestations are not the work of the Spirit of God. For the Spirit of God is the Spirit of Christ.

The Real Purpose of the "*charismata*"

As we have seen before, this leads us quite naturally to a test that can be applied to the presence and use of the *charismata* in the church.

> 9. According to 1 Corinthians 14:26, what must be the purpose of the use of the gifts of the Spirit in a community?

The Greek word for "edification" is *oikodome*, which is the term used for building a house or any other facility.

> 10. According to Ephesians 4:12–14, what is the goal toward which a proper use of the *charismata* should be bringing us ever closer?

True spiritual unity in the knowledge of Christ must be the goal and tendency of every proper use of our spiritual gifts.

CHAPTER 10: DISCERNING THE SPIRIT

11. According to Romans 16:17, what is one of the symptoms of false teaching in spiritual matters?

"I urge you, brothers to watch out for those who:

_____

that are contrary _____"

Let God be God!

God's Spirit is a *person*. Jesus said of the Spirit: He is "the Spirit of truth. The world cannot accept him… But you know him, for he lives with you and will be in you." (John 14:17) The Spirit is the personal Comforter and Counselor for every person who knows the Lord. It is a terrible error, then, to associate the Holy Spirit with any kind of power that can be manipulated by any human technique or formula. In certain forms of mysticism, a type of "spiritual energy" can be released by the touch of a teacher or *guru*. The Holy Spirit is not like this; he is not a parcel of power that we dispense or over whom we have jurisdiction. He is a powerful Person who rules over *us*!

Acts 8:18–24 describes an incident in which Simon, a Samaritan wonderworker, tried to buy the power to impart the Holy Spirit.

12. What was the sin of Simon? (Acts 8:20)

13. What did Simon's way of thinking about the Holy Spirit indicate? (Acts 8:21, 23)

14. What did Peter tell Simon he needed to do? (Acts 8:22)

The Holy Spirit of God is not similar to any kind of "magical" power. He cannot be passed from one person to another by touch, like the "spiritual energy" found in some forms of mysticism. He is the *gift* of God and the expression of God's power to and through those who place their trust in the Name of Jesus. Whenever we think that the Holy Spirit can be bestowed by human agency or even that we are in control of dispensing the Holy Spirit, something has gone wildly astray in our thinking. This is an additional criterion with which to gauge all spiritual phenomena. True spiritual experience is always accompanied by humble reverence toward God.

Growth

"*Oikodome*" (edification) is the process that takes place when a spiritual gift is properly used. The Body of Christ is built up to a genuine unity of spirit. But the principle of "building up" others is not just something for the church. It applies to every area of our lives.

15. Think through your life and ask yourself the question: What could I be doing to "build up" those around me – to encourage them and help them to become more complete and whole people in Christ?

In my family:

With my friends:

In my church or spiritual community:

CHAPTER 10: DISCERNING THE SPIRIT

Wisdom

With the Bible and the "mothers and fathers" of the faith we affirm: all truth comes alone from God. Evil has no independent existence; it can only live as a parasite – as a perversion of good. A lie cannot exist in and of itself; it can only distort the truth. Therefore, wherever life and truth come to light, we see evidence of God's hand. Through this biblical insight, an opportunity for dialogue with the natural sciences, the humanities and even other religions presents itself. But clear, hard thinking is necessary for this task. Many today are saying that we urgently need to develop a new relationship to creation and to our own existence as created beings and they are right. But in so doing *we must not blur the distinction between God's work in creation and his work in salvation.* Attempting to do this is the "original sin" of theology. The "insight" that elements of truth can be found in other religions and spiritual ways should not surprise Christians. The Spirit of Jesus is also the Creator Spirit (and apart from that, some religions borrowed much from the revelation given to Israel and the Church of Jesus Christ). "*Wherever we encounter the truth He is there!*" However, this fact must not lead to the erroneous conclusion: "If that is the way it is, then the whole concept of our need for salvation is obsolete."

On the one hand, we need to do all we can to support the rediscovery of the Triune God as the God of creation; on the other hand, we must not mix up God's work in creation with his work in salvation. Otherwise we're liable to wander away from the Light and end up in a spiritual shadowland in which everything becomes indistinct and muddled… in a spiritual twilight zone in which "every cat is colored gray".

God works both in *creation* and in *salvation*, but these two works of God are not to be viewed as the same. Why not? – because *the sin of humanity* stands between God's work in creation and his work in salvation. In the language of Genesis 3, if our ancestors had *not* eaten from the tree of knowledge of good and evil in the primordial Garden – if they had been satisfied with the fruit from the tree of life, then

GIVER OF GIFTS

the *special* work of God – his work through the cross of Jesus Christ – would not have been necessary. God's Spirit would have dwelt in humanity as a part of his work as *Creator*. But now the chasm is there and our responsibility is to proclaim and teach the salvation work of God in Christ Jesus in the power of the Holy Spirit, with words and signs, until he comes again to redeem all of creation. That means that the death of Jesus Christ for our sin, his resurrection, and his work in saving humanity from our sins must be proclaimed in the marketplace of the world. "Creation spirituality" can never substitute for God's saving work in Christ.

We return once again to that which we observed in Chapter 2: The Spirit of God connects *God's work in creation* with *his work in salvation*. God created the universe from nothing and he sustains it in existence by his will and power. *God's work in salvation* is that which God undertakes to bring all people back into a personal relationship with himself. God is the one who acts in both – particularly through the Holy Spirit! But his activity in each is different.

We have reached the end of our study of the biblical teaching on the person of the Holy Spirit. But this is just the beginning. The *reality* of the Spirit is the path to experiencing the presence of the Triune God; our knowledge *about* him will always be imperfect, though, until we see God face to face!

CHAPTER 10: DISCERNING THE SPIRIT

An ancient prayer of the Church expresses the deep longing of God's People for the reality of the Holy Spirit:

COME, Holy Ghost, our souls inspire,
  And lighten with celestial fire.
  Thou the anointing Spirit art,
  Who dost thy sevenfold gifts impart.
  Thy blessed unction from above,
  Is comfort, life, and fire of love.
  Enable with perpetual light
  The dullness of our blinded sight.
  Anoint and cheer our soiled face
  With the abundance of thy grace.
  Keep far our foes, give peace at home;
  Where thou art guide, no ill can come.
  Teach us to know the Father, Son,
  And thee, of both, to be but One;
  That, through the ages all along,
  This may be our endless song:
  Praise to thy eternal merit,
  Father, Son, and Holy Spirit.
  Amen.

Anglican *Book of Common Prayer*

INDEX

TOPICS

BIBLICAL PASSAGES

"Philosophia International"

This handbook about the Holy Spirit is published by *Philosophia International*.

Philosophia was founded in 2004 by Dr. Clark and Ann Peddicord with a team of friends in the U.S. and Europe as a world-wide community of men and women from different denominations and churches who are followers of Jesus. They share the firm conviction that in a world of conflict and confusion, the message of Jesus provides people of all faiths and none an orientation point for life. Jesus' life, death, and resurrection are the basis for a genuine relationship to the Eternal and a new life.

Philosophia exists to encourage and support the next generation to take active responsibility for the future. *Philosophia* wants to provide tools, opportunities and community to people in every culture who want a different kind of world and are seeking spiritual depth, dialogue and a transforming vision for society and the church. We want to be a community with a clear center in Christ but with "open borders".

We believe that, through the work of God's Spirit, this can open the door for friendship and reconciliation between individuals, groups and nations.

For more information see:
www.philosophia.org
www.philosophia.net (German)

Made in the USA
Columbia, SC
02 June 2021